Praise for
Shopper Intimacy

"Retailers have long had an advantage influencing the customer experience, and today the advantage grows with improved access to individual customer data. *Shopper Intimacy* is a wonderful book to help brands and retailers understand how to excel in engaging and winning consumers and increasing sales."

—**Tom Collinger**, Associate Dean,
Medill School at Northwestern University, and Department Chair,
Integrated Marketing Communications

"With the evolving channel landscape continuing to get more complex, Rick DeHerder and Dick Blatt make an incredible drive to organize both a practical guide to shopper marketing while providing new quantitative insights, approaches, and tools to effectively define shopper marketing ROI versus a soft, qualitative approach. Having spent half my career in the shopper marketing world, not only do DeHerder and Blatt have the global depth and experience in the industry, but they also have highly tuned analytical minds that drive a unique curiosity to get at what is the best method to apply new, actionable metrics to the shopper experience. I highly recommend this book."

—**Bill Kolb**, President and Chief Operating Officer,
MRM Worldwide

"Think global—act local. The authors are real global players and the top experts in retail marketing. Use their experience and insights for your success in store. Transfer global insights into local results."

—**Bert Ohnemueller**, Managing Director, Neuromerchandising
Group, Europe, and Past Chairman, POPAI Europe

"This book is an excellent contribution to build more skilled, intelligent, and useful marketing at retail."

—**Rafael Sampaio**, Executive Vice-President, Association of
Brazilian Advertisers, Executive Committee Member,
World Federation of Advertisers,
and Founder Member, POPAI Brazil

"Two scarred, but well-decorated veterans deconstruct in-store marketing. Rick DeHerder and Dick Blatt give us a tour of where the rubber meets the road in modern consumption. Comprehensive, exhaustive, and complete, this is a volume for both marketer and merchant."

—**Paco Underhill**, Founder, CEO, and President, Envirosell and Author of *What Women Want, Why We Buy,* and *Call of the Mall*

"Enhancing our in-store environment with relevant products, promotions, and innovations *will* win shopper loyalty. That loyalty will drive more shoppers, greater baskets, and more trips, leading to incremental revenue and market share for Walgreens. *Shopper Intimacy* is a fantastic resource for time-poor marketing professionals seeking insights, interpretations, and implications of the vast library of research and studies in the field of in-store marketing. Additionally, this guide will help us make better decisions on our marketing spending by providing a structured approach and the necessary metrics for calculating a return on that spend."

—**Don Whetsone**, Senior Director of Merchandising Strategy and Development, Walgreens

SHOPPER INTIMACY

SHOPPER INTIMACY

A PRACTICAL GUIDE TO LEVERAGING MARKETING INTELLIGENCE TO DRIVE RETAIL SUCCESS

Rick DeHerder and Dick Blatt

© 2011 by Pearson Education, Inc.
Publishing as FT Press
Upper Saddle River, New Jersey 07458

FT Press offers excellent discounts on this book when ordered in quantity for bulk purchases or special sales. For more information, please contact U.S. Corporate and Government Sales, 1-800-382-3419, corp-sales@pearsontechgroup.com.

For sales outside the U.S., please contact International Sales at international@pearson.com.

Printed in the United States of America

ISBN-10: 0-13-707543-X
ISBN-13: 978-0-13-707543-0

First Printing September 2010

Pearson Education LTD.
Pearson Education Australia PTY, Limited.
Pearson Education Singapore, Pte. Ltd.
Pearson Education North Asia, Ltd.
Pearson Education Canada, Ltd.
Pearson Educación de Mexico, S.A. de C.V.
Pearson Education—Japan
Pearson Education Malaysia, Pte. Ltd.

The Library of Congress cataloging-in-publication data is on file.

Vice President, Publisher
Tim Moore

Associate Publisher and Director of Marketing
Amy Neidlinger

Acquisions Editor
Megan Colvin

Operations Manager
Gina Kanouse

Senior Marketing Manager
Julie Phifer

Publicity Manager
Laura Czaja

Assistant Marketing Manager
Megan Colvin

Cover Designer
Alan Clements

Managing Editor
Kristy Hart

Project Editors
Jovana San Nicolas-Shirley and Barbara Campbell

Copy Editor
San Dee Phillips

Proofreader
Seth Kerney

Indexer
Erika Millen

Compositor
Jake McFarland

Manufacturing Buyer
Dan Uhrig

To Sharon and Sue

Contents

Introduction 1

Chapter 1   REAP (Retail Ecosystem Analytics Process)........... 7

Utilizing REAP to Deliver Consistent Results.............................. 7

Shopper Analysis Integration 12

Case Studies.. 17

Chapter 2   Measuring Marketing at Retail in
Supermarkets... 25

Overview... 25

Phase One—POPAI's Channel Studies............................. 26

Chapter 3   Measuring Marketing at Retail in
Convenience Stores 43

Overview... 43

Learning One: Retail Marketing Execution Techniques
Concentrated 47

Learning Two: Marketing Messages Concentrated 48

Learning Three: Huge Premium for Excellence.......................... 49

Learning Four: Brand Size Drives Outpost Display Activity 50

Learning Five: Category Response Varies Widely by
Message Location 51

Learning Six: Borrowed Interest Has a Disproportionate
Impact on Smaller Brands... 52

Learning Seven: Strong Brand Expression Significantly
Outperforms Generic Treatment................................. 53

Learning Eight: Store Is Not Overloaded with
Retail Marketing Material 53

Learning Nine: Effectiveness Ratio Predicts Sales Success 55

Learning Ten: Retailer Analysis Yields Success
sImplementation Model.. 56

Chapter 4   Measuring Marketing at Retail in Drug Stores.....63

Overview 63

Learning One: Many Key Results Consistent with
Other Studies 64

Learning Two: Retail Marketing Effectiveness Higher in
Chain Drug Stores 65

Learning Three: Message Matters 65

Learning Four: Promotion/Advertising Consistently
Enhances Impact 68

Learning Five: Brand-Focused Messages More Effective 70

Learning Six: Price Savings Drive Impulse Results 72

Learning Seven: Value Message Drives Private Label 72

Learning Eight: Shopper Actions Differ from Words 74

Learning Nine: RFID Tracking Delivers Reliable,
Real-Time Data 74

Learning Ten: Retail Audience and CPM Very Attractive 75

Chapter 5   Establishing In-Store Marketing Measures 79

Retail Marketing Metrics 79

Definitions 79

Potential Reach 81

Actual Audience Reach 82

In-Store Rating Points 82

Cost Per Thousand (CPM) 83

Audience Delivery Worksheet 84

Phase One Summary 85

Phase Two—Nielsen's PRISM Project 89

Research Learnings 93

Summary 96

Chapter 6   Capturing Shopping Dynamics in Store 101

Overview 101

Market Tests 103

Examples of Retail Marketing Ratios 110

Potential Applications 116

Recap 117

Summary 119

The Retail Marketing Model Shifts 120

Chapter 7 **Shopper Models** 125

Retail Marketing Definition 125

Shopper Understanding... 126

Summary 143

Chapter 8 **Decision Drivers** 145

Retail Factors and Purchase Decision Types 145

Financial Impact of Presentation Optimization 145

Retail Success Drivers 150

Leveraging Related Items.. 177

Shaping Opportunities 187

Emotional Power.. 188

Practical Learnings... 191

Summary 194

Chapter 9 **Online Retailing** 197

Applying Learning and Traditional Tools 197

Managing Online Dynamics.. 207

Online Tools 208

Chapter 10 **Measuring Return on Investment** 215

Delivering Results 215

Retail Tools.. 219

Return on Investment Models 223

Achieving Success Through Shopper Intimacy......................... 229

Index.. 235

Acknowledgments

Our book is based on the unique perspectives we gained from experience in the nonprofit world, where you can see firsthand how an entire industry functions and how various companies approach their business differently, and from the for-profit world, with direct experience in multiple shareholder settings—retail, brand, and supply side.

We are indebted to the work with our colleagues at POPAI—The Global Association for Marketing at Retail, whose preliminary studies of our industry informed some of our judgments and, at the same time, made clear the need for this book. We especially acknowledge the POPAI Board of Directors who recognized and acted upon the need for much more research for the medium over a decade ago.

It has been our good fortune to have met and worked with many of the most thoughtful and creative leaders in our industry—brilliant advertising executives, academics, and industry consultants, whose collective work has shaped the thinking of our industry. We cite them throughout this book to give them full credit for their hard work and innovative thinking.

We add a word of thanks to our friend Jim Spaeth of Sequent Partners, who through the years has always been available to provide insight into industry research and solid strategic guidance. And also a word of thanks to Ralph Oman, former head of the U.S. Copyright Office and now at George Washington University School of Law, for his review and guidance on the appropriate citing of the many sources of information shared in the book.

We would also like to recognize the contributions of the primary researchers for much of the field work, including Doug Adams of Prime Consulting, Inc., Martin Kingdon of Sheridan Global Consulting, and the team at Nielsen In Store.

Lastly, we are both indebted to our wives, Sharon and Sue, who have patiently tolerated our world travels as we built a wealth of experience in, knowledge of, and insight into the marketing at retail industry. We endeavor to share that knowledge with you here and hope you find it useful.

Rick DeHerder
Dick Blatt

About the Authors

The authors have a deep involvement in the industry with complementary backgrounds. They collaborated to lead a great deal of the primary industry research and together have worked with the leaders of every industry segment. They are uniquely positioned to use their familiarity with the industry and the research to apply their personal experience to create a comprehensive review of marketing at retail with a guide for driving retail success.

Rick DeHerder was the founder of Array, a leading designer and manufacturer of fixtures and displays, with operations in North America and China and a network of strategic partners around the world. Prior to founding Array in 1999, Rick spent 24 years in both brand marketing as Executive Vice President at Mattel, and in the retail industry at Sears, working in the stores, regional offices, and headquarters. This broad-based experience gives him unique insight into the challenges of retail marketing at all levels.

Dick Blatt is the president of Planar World Consulting. He served as the CEO of POPAI—The Global Association for Marketing at Retail, for 17 years. In this role, he was called upon to author articles and deliver presentations around the world on the subject of marketing at retail, its future, and its trends. He was also selected to provide The Center for Association Leadership with two case studies of excellence for going global and reinventing the association.

During his tenure, one of the association's primary strategic goals was to integrate the marketing at retail medium in the strategic marketing mix. The association also expanded to include 20 country chapters, with an organizational presence on every populated continent.

Introduction

Intimacy is the only sustainable path to consistent results.

The marketing world is in the midst of unprecedented changes that shatter the core of all the traditional, "proven" marketing models. The changes retailers and marketers confront extend far beyond the well-documented implosion of traditional media to include both consumers and retailers. Quite simply, every part of the conventional world is in flux with new models yet to be defined. Increasingly, it appears that Moore's Law, which postulates that processing capacity will double every two years, can easily be applied to marketing to describe the speed of change and innovation. Achieving and maintaining, not just a connection, but true intimacy with the shopper, is the new necessity.

Why do we say shopper intimacy?

Today, although more attention than ever is focused on understanding what motivates the shopper, the conversation generally revolves around, shopper insights. We suggest that having insights into your shoppers buying habits is not enough.

For true success, you need intimacy—understanding what your shopper does and is going to do in this shopping environment and why. With this knowledge, you can better tailor and deliver both your message and offer to encourage trial and long-term brand loyalty.

Shopper intimacy comes from knowing how shoppers actually behave at retail as revealed in the extensive in-store research, applying psychology and cognitive behavior studies to these observations to understand the motivation for these behaviors, and then rigorously applying these learnings throughout the organization in a formal program we call the Retail Ecosystem Analytics Process (REAP).

Three macro-trends with profound implications for retailers and marketers drive the current market shifts—major demographic shifts, media changes, and the maturation of dominant retail concepts. Together these trends have initiated unprecedented and ever-accelerating change that affects all of us.

Demographically, we live in an older society with more concentrated wealth and smaller households that increasingly do not meet the definition of a traditional family. Additionally, a series of dramatic shifts between the older and younger generations can be seen in the growing multiculturalism of society and the rapid adoption of new technologies by the youngest members of society. The generations meet in their increasing consumption of services versus goods, but diverge in their understanding of the personal implications of technology.

Together these trends explode the now antiquated notion of a mass market and destroy the utility of measuring efforts to reach consumers in terms of cost per thousand. The rapid adoption of transformative technologies amplifies the demographic trends so that new consumers increasingly self-define the groups with which they identify and assert control over the information they consume and choices they make. The new consumers expect to find any product in the place they want to purchase it. They expect universal quality and low costs. They want products and shopping venues that speak to them as individuals and members of the groups they create and select.

These demographic trends extend to traditional media decimated by the effects of these shifts. The net is the delivery of fewer consumers for a constantly rising cost through a business model that may not be sustainable as advertisers demand accountability for all expenditures. This focus on accountability extends to every element of the marketing plan and means that marketers need to know what their shoppers had the opportunity to see, what they actually saw, and whether that interaction culminated in a sale.

In the retail world, the dominant shopping formats have matured and expanded across the developed geographies so that the metric for developed markets is now same-store sales, and store count growth is predominantly driven by expansion in developing economies. The focus on same-store sales performance results in assortment expansion into high-traffic categories to spur more store visits and the growth of private labels to capture higher margins per transaction. As with media, each investment is tested against its return to the bottom line.

The inter-related strands of shopper diversification and empowerment, mass media implosion, and retail maturation converging at a time of great economic distress creates a major inflection point that shifts more attention to the marketing activity at retail.

Unfortunately, although leading practitioners recognize these shifts, they also acknowledge that their organizations lack crucial pieces of understanding in the areas that are most critical to driving greater success in the marketing at retail arena. These leading practitioners agree on an ideal model in which marketing research and insights generated from a steady stream of measurement data and performance metrics for retail lead to the development and execution of well-defined strategies that engage shoppers, close sales, and ultimately create the brand loyalty that underpins brand equity (see Figure I.1). At the same time, they ruefully admit that they are unable to effectively execute against it.

Marketing-at-Retail Model

Figure I.1 REAP Design Process

This book seeks to provide the data, tools, and methodology that provide the missing links for implementing this model and increasing retail success.

Our shopper intimacy program promises to bring together the worlds of retailers and marketers in the place where they meet with the shopper. Intimacy drives consistent retail results, and to achieve intimacy, we take a journey in five phases:

- Market intelligence on shopper behavior at retail
- Behavioral research to unlock the foundational precepts driving shopping behavior in store
- A process for integrating this data to achieve intimacy with the shopper
- Tools for implementing strategies driven by this intimacy
- New measurement techniques for tracking success

Collectively, the industry has spent millions of dollars on research in-store to

- Quantify the traffic in the store
- Track the marketing activity taking place at retail
- Measure the impact of differential executions in different channels
- Track shoppers interaction with marketing material and its eventual conversion into sales

If shopper intimacy provides the path to consistent results, the knowledge gained from research at retail provides the necessary information base for its initiation. We dissect the recent market intelligence with an eye to drawing lessons about what works at retail by measuring shoppers' behavior in stores. We then move to a discussion of key academic research into shopper behavior, breaking our review into the biologic, cognitive, logical, and social foundations of human behavior in the retail environment. By applying the knowledge developed by researchers in the lab with the intelligence gathered in-store, we establish a contextual framework through which we can isolate key variables to create insights. By testing and verifying insights within a formal process and setting up a continuous feedback cycle, we create intimacy with the shoppers as we answer the fundamental question of what shoppers want (see Figure I.2).

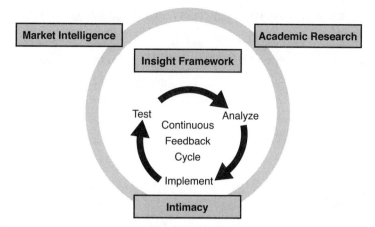

Figure I.2 Shopper Analysis - Integration

As with any program, strategy without execution results in complete failure. To ensure that our hard-won intimacy drives results, we developed a Retail Ecosystem Analytics Process (REAP) that extends strategic consideration to all the key players in creating retail success. Combined with the tools developed from our analyses of successful programs, we provide a practical guide to generating ongoing sales success (see Figure I.3).

Figure I.3 REAP Strategy

The payoff is the information, tools, and methodology to deliver the following:

- Better understanding of the marketing at retail environment
- Improved retail results based on insights that lead to shopper intimacy
- Establishment of a more accurate medium valuation
- Proper integration of retail into marketing mix

John Wanamaker, the much-admired 19th-century merchant, famously said, "I know half the money I spend on advertising is wasted.... I just don't know which half." Our studies help lift this veil of mystery to understand what works and why, so we can better predict what will work in the future to drive increased marketing investment efficiency.

1

REAP (Retail Ecosystem Analytics Process)

The research and analyses detailed throughout this book provide valuable data on how shoppers behave in stores and why. But, without a defined means of transforming that data into insights and action plans that are implemented, the data is of marginal value. Implementing REAP (Retail Ecosystem Analytics Process) is central to the development of the shopper intimacy that drives consistent results.

Utilizing REAP to Deliver Consistent Results

The key elements of REAP are

- Use of data and analyses to define targets

- Focus on servicing the defined shopper's needs

- Translation of the targeted shopper needs into strategy and action plans

- Full involvement of all the retail marketing disciplines

- Continuous feedback and analysis to refine and enhance future executions

The successful implementation of REAP requires

- Analyses of the retail opportunity from all angles

- Definition and segmentation of opportunities for analyses and development

- Implementation of formal procedures for delivering consistent results

Analysis

REAP begins with a thorough analysis in which we mine the existing data, segment our targeted shoppers, and then develop the ideal positioning to best serve the targeted segments. The data mining includes an examination of all the available information sources including syndicated data, loyalty cards, house credit cards, in-store studies, and focus group research. We use that data to develop a profile of the various customer segments that shop our locations and then focus on the segments we want to develop as a point of focus. This segmentation, when combined with the research analyses, unearths the key drivers for the most desirable segments and the ideal positioning to best serve targeted customers' needs.

Assortment

With our positioning goal in place, we define our product, establish product groupings that support the targeted shopping groups' objectives in visiting our stores, and then organize these groupings for efficient shopping. Our product definition includes an understanding of the items that shoppers need to complete their shopping mission. Proper product grouping leverages the shift from a passive journey through the store to an active purchase consideration so that related items are seen, evaluated, and purchased. Well-executed organization optimizes the return generated from each customers' visit by directing customers through a shopping path that supports the efficient completion of their tasks in our store.

Structure

Next we structure our conversation with shoppers by guiding them from a general orientation to an eventual purchase decision. At a macro level we design the flow of the store to guide their navigation through the physical space with appropriate graphics and signposts. Understanding that shoppers predominantly follow the path we establish, we want to reward their choice by making our flow and navigation intuitive in anticipating their needs on this shopping mission. At the same time, we want to create a controlled interruption of the potentially rote shopping expedition to generate incremental revenue. The graphics and guideposts we employ should support the shopping process on multiple levels (logical, emotional, and so on) and reduce shopper's stress level by providing the right type of information so that they are open to more of our marketing messages.

Design

The design process encompasses all the executional elements of the plan including the architecture, store lighting, and merchandising fixtures. Each of these is designed to support the strategic goal of anticipating shopper needs and facilitating their purchase decisions (see Figure 1.1).

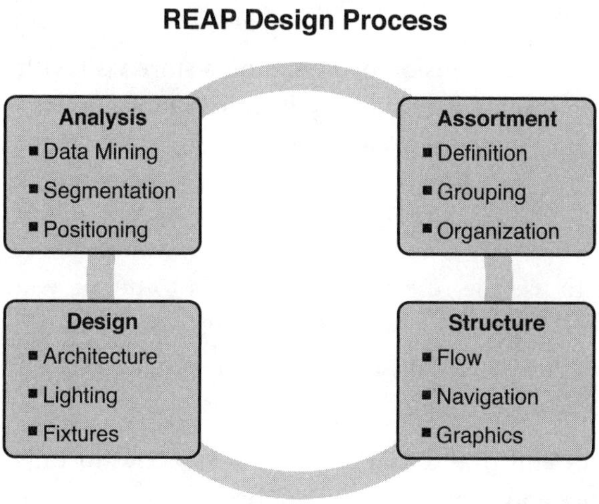

REAP Design Process

Analysis	Assortment
■ Data Mining	■ Definition
■ Segmentation	■ Grouping
■ Positioning	■ Organization

Design	Structure
■ Architecture	■ Flow
■ Lighting	■ Navigation
■ Fixtures	■ Graphics

Figure 1.1 REAP Design Process

Constituency Inclusion

Throughout the design process, the shopper is at the center of our thought universe. However, we must also understand the needs and input from all the participants in the retail marketing equation: retailers, brands, and agencies.

As we refine our shopper analysis and develop a profile of our targeted shopper segments, we must recognize that the behavior of defined groups within stores will vary based on a variety of factors associated with the specific shopping occasion such as the shopping objective;

(major shopping trip or fill-in visit) or the addition of others to the shopping party (spouse, friend, child, and so on).

For example, if we target harried young mothers and seek to build store loyalty, we may want to

- Utilize an entrance area for quick meals on the go—she can quickly pass through the area on her major shopping trips, but will appreciate the convenience if she wants to pick up a meal on her way home from work or a family event.

- Add special check-out lanes with a kid-friendly/mom-approved product assortment in identified lanes to remove a potential irritant.

- Reward the inclusion of a child on a store visit with a small gift so that the youngest family members look forward to the visit and family shopping becomes a pleasant experience (also understanding that shoppers with children tend to purchase more than those without children).

The key is to use the research and analyses to define your most valued shoppers' segments and understand their needs on different visits. Armed with this understanding, build your programs to anticipate and meet those needs.

For agencies and brand marketers, it is essential to fully appreciate retailer issues and goals. Retailers are oriented toward a consideration of brands based on what they can provide in terms of

- Influencing the shopper's choice of channel and specific retailer

- Driving the shopper's choice of shopping outlet

- Impact on store positioning and store brand promise

- Effect on total category purchases

Agencies and marketers must further appreciate the different concerns of the multiple constituencies within the retailer. They must understand the interplay between brands within and between related segments. Winning programs focus on driving total store or total category sales versus trading dollars within the store or category.

Retailers and agencies must, likewise, fully appreciate brand objectives to be met at retail. They must evaluate and understand the interplay between channel preferences for brand purchases and the impact brands have on the total shopping basket. They must also appreciate the differing needs of the constituencies within brand organizations. Winning retailers leverage the power of the brand as a thought and labor-saving tool for shoppers in store so that shoppers are less fatigued and open to increasing the total size of their basket.

Agencies must work to understand the essential dynamics in store. They need to be a knowledge center for the intersection of the key players in the fulfillment of the shopper's needs. They then need to apply creativity to the expression of the marketing programs that support important retail and brand goals while facilitating the shopper's mission in store. Finally, they guide the implementation of the program through the involved constituencies and their intermediaries.

All parties work separately and together to deepen their insights and their relationships with consumers and shoppers. The development of this relationship includes

- Qualitative and quantitative analysis
- Understanding shopper dynamics by channel, outlet, segment, and shopping occasion
- The key drivers of the fall-off between intent and action
- Proprietary and syndicated research

Retailers possess a unique information source in their ownership of transaction data and shopper trip/household behavior from proprietary databases through loyalty and credit card programs; brands own singular data sources in their experience with multiple retailers and channels, and their proprietary research on customer interaction and preferences with brands and discrete product segments; agencies control a particular knowledge base with their work across brand and retail categories and their immersion in multiple geographies and grasp of the technical specifics of the marketing disciplines essential to successful program execution. Our ability to make sound marketing decisions is constrained by our access to relevant data and knowledge. Cooperation and collaboration dramatically increases the available knowledge and data improving our planning and the results they generate. This collaboration among the retail marketing resources should be a foregone conclusion.

In our early days in the industry, Mel Korn was a passionate advocate for collaboration among retailers, brands, agencies, and marketing at retail producers to optimize at-store campaigns—a point that seemed obvious. We did not fully appreciate the need for the advocacy until a chance conversation highlighted the norm for how programs were generally executed.

A display honored as the best of the year by POPAI, the industry's non-profit trade association, delivered a forceful brand message while also displaying the product beautifully. It was truly attention grabbing with bright colors, creative design and greatly increased ease of access to the product. Additionally, the fixture perfectly integrated with the general media campaign.

Upon congratulating the fixture producer, we were shocked when he burst into laughter and shared that the integration relied totally on a chance meeting with the general media agency in the client's hallway. As the fixture producer was on his way to meet with the purchasing department, he gathered bits of information in a two-minute conversation with his agency counterparts who had just met with the brand team.

By sheer circumstance and skilled follow-up, they captured the essence of the TV ads in the retail campaign to drive a program that was a creative and business success.

Shopper Analysis Integration

Today, integrated programs routinely integrate key data sources so that marketers can optimize their retail efforts. In this integrated process, they combine data from proprietary sources such as transactional data, loyalty programs, credit cards, advertising/promotional effectiveness tracking, shopping pattern analysis, electronic marketing results, and so on with external data such as ethnographic overlays, syndicated research (MARI, channel studies, and such), geographic/ trade zone maps, brand partner databases and insights, and more.

This data is then analyzed to identify meaningful patterns and groupings. Further analysis of the clusters leads to the segmentation of actionable shopper groups based on profitability.

Cluster analysis informs a series of strategic decisions that drives subsequent choices related to assortment, adjacencies, planograms, store navigation, and so on (see Figure 1.2).

Shopper Analysis–Integration

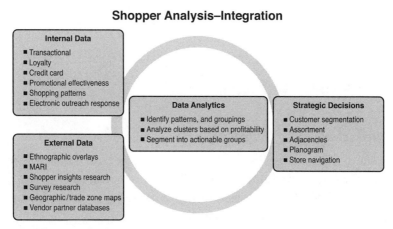

Figure 1.2 Shopper Analysis Integration

In completing their analysis, retailers may access syndicated research, account team interviews, store associate interviews, shopping basket diagnostics, current program reviews, competitive situation analyses, and retail audits. Brands may supplement these efforts with their own shopping basket analyses, reviews of their current program results, a trade-off analysis of the costs and benefits of alternative strategies, and insights from the syndicated and proprietary research to which they have access. Uniting these efforts creates synergy that increases program impact as compared to individually generated programs. Retail success is driven by traffic and transaction value. By involving agencies, brands, and retailers in the strategic discussion of how best to meet shoppers' needs within a formal process that includes assortment, structure, and design, we significantly increase the impact and effectiveness of our programs (see Figure 1.3).

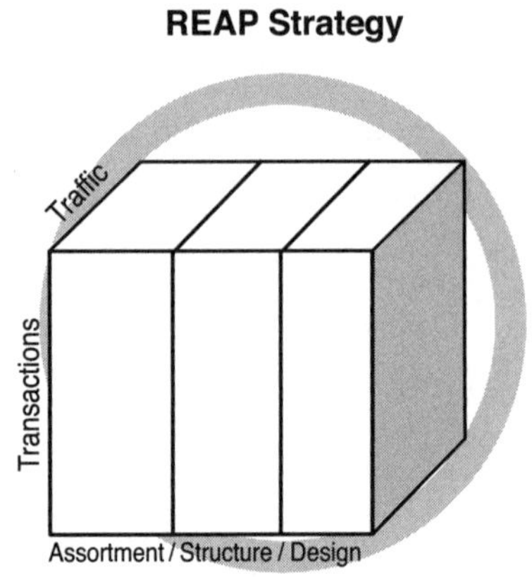

REAP Strategy

Figure 1.3 REAP Strategy

Retail Marketing Scorecards

By routinely measuring results and analyzing campaigns within a formal process, we generate important insights that can improve results for future programs. The inclusion of academic research at the biologic, cognitive, logical, and social levels yields even more nuanced analyses and insight (see Figure 1.4).

Shopper Relevancy Scorecard

	Biologic	Cognitive	Logical	Social
M@R A				
M@R B				
M@R C				
M@R D				

Figure 1.4 Shopper Relevancy Scorecard

Likewise, we can examine the likely acceptance of the program by the various constituencies within the brand marketing organization (see Figure 1.5).

We can further consider our proposed program in terms of its likely implementation at retail by looking beyond the headquarters teams to appraise its acceptance by the field operations team and the floor personnel (see Figure 1.6).

Brand Acceptance Scorecard

	Mktg	Sales	DSD
M@R A			
M@R B			
M@R C			
M@R D			

Figure 1.5 Brand Acceptance Scorecard

Retailer Acceptance Scorecard

	Strat	Ops	Floor
M@R A			
M@R B			
M@R C			
M@R D			

Figure 1.6 Retailer Acceptance Scorecard

Integrating all these considerations, we maximize our odds of success and the likely impact of our program by evaluating programs against a holistic scorecard (see Figure 1.7).

Holistic Marketing Program Scorecard

	Biologic	Cognitive	Logical	Social	Mktg	Sales	DSD	Strat	Ops	Floor
M@R A										
M@R B										
M@R C										
M@R D										

Figure 1.7 Holistic Marketing Scorecard

Segmentation Premiums

As we develop our strategy we recognize that, for retailing, the great middle has been lost with the death of the old homogenous mass markets. We operate in an environment that rewards the outstanding service of important, defined market segments and punishes the generic pursuit of a generalized middle ground (see Figure 1.8). The premium associated with excellence in specialization is evident in space productivity measures and comparative stock valuations. For instance, Whole Food delivers sales per square foot of $882[1] and a stock valued at a five-year average price earnings ratio of 42.7[2] versus Kroger's $466 per square foot[3] and a price earnings ratio generally in the 11 to 12 range.[4]

M@R Strategy

Figure 1.8 Retail Marketing Strategy

Successfully identifying the segments you cultivate is a critical component of retail success deserving of careful consideration. Many standards have been used for shopper segmentation including demographic, ethnographic, psychographic, and usage criteria. Often, marketers combine traits to describe unique groups to be targeted based on a combination of characteristics that translates into a distinct profile. A key consideration when building targeted groups is that they must be meaningful aggregations that are discrete; that is, uniquely different from each other so that each shopper is placed in one group versus multiple segments. We must also reach the identified groupings so that the plans developed are actionable. Brands should segment their channels to service their customers across the shopping universe and then collaborate with retailers within each channel. Successful collaboration yields sales increases whereas breakdowns result in lost opportunities.

Traditional Shopper Segmentation Traits

- Size
- Growth
- Composition
- Demographics
- Leisure pursuits

- Influencer versus follower
- Shopper versus user
- Shopping purpose
- Visit frequency

Case Studies

The following examples illustrate the application of these principles. The samples chosen illustrate the interplay of various elements of REAP to drive strategy formation and execution in the store.

Retailer Assortment Rationalization

A project with a major discounter provides a case study for the use of shopper segmentation to support strategic assortment decisions to increase revenue and profit. Working with category management teams from leading brands, the chain began to define the specific shopping segments it wanted to nurture and develop and then analyze the role different categories played in reaching that segment and supporting total chain profitability. The teams quickly focused on families with children as the most profitable segment. Data showed that this group visited the channel most frequently and spent the most money. Deeper analyses showed that the particular retailer was doing the worst job among key competitors in reaching this segment.

	HH with Children	HH without Children
Trip Frequency	115	92
Dollars Spent	136	81

Focusing on this broadly defined target, the teams then studied the contents of shopping baskets for different items and categories. The team identified that a basket with detergent in it averaged eight items; the biggest shopping basket contained an item of children's apparel; the second biggest basket had a toy in it; and, the most valuable shopping basket with a toy in it included a Barbie doll. By contrast a transaction with a case of motor oil was generally purchased by a man shopping

---

alone, and the predominant share of transactions contained motor oil and nothing else.

Prior to the analysis, motor oil was featured in every weekly circular and held a prominent in-store display location. The marketing teams evaluated motor oil against the number of transactions and direct revenue generated from the ad. The thinking had been, even though the item was generally advertised as a loss, it generated tremendous traffic that yielded significant sales dollars. When this perspective was broadened to the total shopping basket, it was clear that oil delivered the wrong kind of traffic and that the category provided a negative impact on total store profitability. As a result, the line was de-emphasized and the advertising was invested in items and categories that would appeal to the newly identified target audience so that the featured items generated sales of other items of interest to the target.

An alternative approach that yielded poor results occurred at a big box general merchant. In an effort to improve profitability, groups, departments, and buyers were challenged to review their areas and make tough assortment decisions on items, categories, and departments based on their profitability. A number of intelligent decisions were made. However, because the shopper was not consistently placed at the center of the process at all levels, for a time a buyer decided to delist tennis balls that had a negative margin while continuing to carry tennis rackets that carried a high margin. The decision did not last long because you could obviously not be credible in the tennis market offering rackets without balls. This decision illustrates how easily bad decisions can be made when the perspective is not properly focused on serving the shopper.

Collaborative Failure

Although the focus on defining a shopper segment and then positioning categories and advertising to meet her needs was a consistent success generator, it did not always translate to all channels in different markets around the world. At Mattel, our analysis showed that roughly 50 percent of total toy sales occurred in the period from January to September and 50 percent from October to December. This ratio held in virtually every developed market around the world, except France. In France, toy distribution is dominated by hypermarkets, and each hypermarket followed a similar strategy in building a large toy presentation for the holiday season and then shrinking it to a small area in January. Beyond that, the channel overwhelmingly stocked these small departments with remnants and did not update the assortment until the subsequent holiday season. As a result, the relative share between the two selling periods was 33 percent and 67 percent.

Armed with the data on the relative value of families with children, the value of different shopping baskets containing items from different categories, and the consistency of shopping patterns from developed markets around the world, we made a compelling case for the competitive opportunity open to the retailer who focused on this segment and leveraged all the categories of interest against the targeted shopper segment to build a preference for their chain. Unfortunately, the argument was not successfully received and a significant opportunity remained unfulfilled.

Brand Channel Segmentation

Just as retailers can apply segmentation analyses to target and develop groups of shoppers, brands can segment and target channels and chains to support their goals for reaching and servicing their customers.

Mattel faced a situation in which the growth and health of its business varied widely by segment. Its specialty business, primarily in doll stores, was strong; however, the mass business broke into an expanding business for its largest accounts, who were growing and capturing share, and a contracting business for the traditional outlets that were losing share. This share loss was across all categories of merchandise as strong regional players gave way to national behemoths. The eventual strategy was to maintain support for the shrinking accounts but recognize that it could not overcome the larger market forces to move into a growth position. Simultaneously, Mattel would work to become more intertwined with driving the total business for the largest accounts while, at the same time, focusing on opening new channels of distribution (see Figure 1.9).

The result was growth in its total business by reaching more customers where they were shopping. The doll store business remained stable while the decline of the traditional accounts was managed.

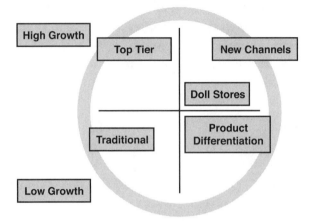

Channel Segmentation

High Growth

Top Tier

New Channels

Doll Stores

Traditional

Product Differentiation

Low Growth

Figure 1.9 Channel Segmentation

Shopper Psychographic Segmentation

In addition to the broad shopper segmentation discussed in the discount store example, we can apply a more detailed shopper segmentation that uses a psychographic profile to identify and target shopper groups. In this type of segmentation, we broaden our view to consider a vast array of possibilities before settling on the key elements that drive performance and drive our strategy.

We begin by identifying a variety of potential traits. The possibilities could number in the hundreds as long as they are identifiable, discrete, measurable, and actionable. Potential distinctions could include attitudes, behaviors, demographics, media habits, and so on. These traits are then tested to isolate the key predictors that drive performance and profitability at retail. Shoppers are then broken into separate clusters with a quantification of their key differences and preferences. This cluster analysis is then utilized to develop retail strategy with an ideal positioning carried through all the key marketing elements inside and outside the store, using the design process previously outlined. The strategy is then implemented with measurement and further refinement (see Figure 1.10).

A hypothetical example from the grocery channel illustrates the process. As a first step, we divide the shoppers who visit our chain into customer segments defined not by demographics but by their relationship to the store. In this analysis we have advocates, who are dedicated to fresh food and shop the chain religiously. They visit at a rate higher than the norm and buy almost all their products from us. Devotees are dedicated to the store and buy most of their needs from us, but they do not shop as frequently as our advocates, and they do not buy as a high a percentage of their total food needs from us. Convenience shoppers purchase select items from us when we fit with their schedule. Deal seekers pore over the weekly circulars and shop our stores when they see items on promotion that fit with their planned purchases for the week. Drop-bys visit the store only occasionally. Figure 1.11 breaks out the percentage of shoppers by category.

Psychographic Segmentation Process

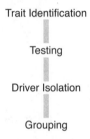

Figure 1.10 Psychographic Segmentation Process

Shopper Segmentation

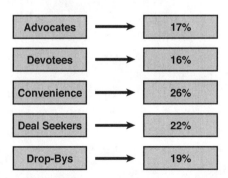

Figure 1.11 Shopper Segmentation

Having identified the relevant shopper segments, we then measure the share of sales and total profit associated with each group. The highly desirable clusters that included advocates, devotees, and convenience shoppers indexed at more than twice the profitability of deal seeker shoppers and drop-bys. The net is that, although the desirable segments represent 59 percent of the market, they deliver 76 percent of total revenue and 86 percent of the profit (see Figure 1.12).

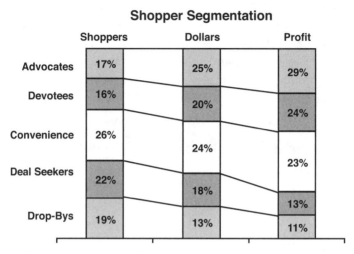

Figure 1.12 Segmentation Profit Impact

From there we define the key retailer attributes that influence the choice of retail outlet for the targeted shopper segments and break the attributes into categories based on their level of importance in the decision-making process, as shown in Figure 1.13. In our example, important retail attributes include freshness, everyday value, quality, check-out speed, and cleanliness. Moderately important features included staff friendliness, assortment, and store location. For the key shoppers, private labels, promotional prices, and sampling were not important. Understanding the factors that mattered most to the shoppers we want to attract and retain, we then measure competitive performance to define areas of excellence and opportunities. With a full understanding of who is important to us, what is important to them, and how they see us in the competitive context, we can build a strategy that resonates with the targeted groups.

Earlier in our analysis we laid out the essential retail marketing dynamic in which performance is a function of the audience we attract, their acceptance of our message, and our persuasiveness in converting the shopper's openness into action.

$$Performance = (Audience \times Acceptance) \times Conversion$$

Store Feature Scoring

		Rating		
		Excellent	Acceptable	Unacceptable
Importance	High	Freshness Everyday Value Quality	Check-out Cleanliness	
	Medium	Friendliness	Assortment Location	Parking
	Low	Private Labels	Promotional Price	Sampling

Figure 1.13 Store Feature Scoring

The acceptance of our marketing and product offerings is a function of the receptivity of the shopper, which is in turn driven by the relevancy of the stimuli we offer and the relaxation of the shopper.

Acceptance ➜ Receptivity = Relevance + Relaxation

By segmenting the universe of potential shoppers into the groups that will drive our profitability and then understanding what is important to these groups and how we stack up against those key drivers, we identify a clear path to a winning strategy that can deliver consistently improved results (see Figure 1.14).

Marketing at Retail Dynamic

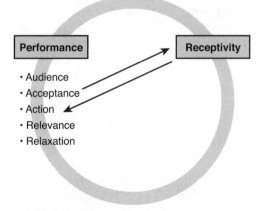

Figure 1.14 Retail Marketing Dynamic

Summary

REAP provides a formal process for translating research into an action plan that delivers sustainable results. The focus on the shopper needs and state of mind throughout the process provides a clear path to the achievement of shopper intimacy. The key elements of a successful REAP implementation are

- Definition of shopper needs

- Use of data analyses to establish targets

- Translation of shopper need by target group into strategy and action plans

- Full involvement of all retail marketing participants

- Continuous feedback and analyses to enhance future programs

Endnotes

1. Whole Foods (2008) *Annual Report*. June 14, 2010, http://www.wholefoodsmarket.com/company/pdfs/ar08.pdf

2. Miriam Marcus, Beyond Low Price-Earnings Ratios, Forbes.com, April 22, 2009. http://www.forbes.com/forbes/2009/0511/050-equity-value-sales-beyond-low-price-earnings.html

3. Kroger (2008) *Annual Report*. June 14, 2010, http://www.thekrogerco.com/finance/documents/2008_KrogerFactBook.pdf

4. http://finapps.forbes.com/finapps/jsp/finance/compinfo/Ratios.jsp?tkr=KR[1]Doug Adams, "POP Measures Up: Learning from the Supermarket Class of Trade", Washington, D.C., POPAI (2001), page 4.

2

Measuring Marketing at Retail in Supermarkets

Overview

Research delivers levels of learning on shopper behavior in store

Although the need for research and actionable information is well accepted now, this was not always the case. In 1998, POPAI established a Measured Medium Initiative with the objective of establishing the store and the realm of retail marketing as a measured medium on par with the traditional media. The association set out to develop a common language for the medium that worked with the lexicon of general advertising, measured the marketing activity in the store, and tracked the shoppers' interactions with products and marketing in store.

Research activity has continued, led by POPAI and then Nielsen, to prove the methodology, deliver learning in specific trade channels, define retail marketing dynamics, and generate the key metrics crucial to the execution of successful retail programs. Collectively, these organizations and the sponsors of the research have spent tens of millions of dollars generating data and insight into the key elements of executing effective campaigns.

Timeline

1998—POPAI establishes Measured Medium Initiative

1999—Methodology Pilot

2000/1—Supermarket Channel Study

2001/2—Convenience Channel Study

2004—Drug Store Channel Study

2006—MARI launched

2007—Nielsen's PRISM and MARI field tests

2008—MARI Refinement

2009— MARI Phase 2

POPAI's overall research project goals were to systematically measure[1]

- Proof of placement
- Cost effectiveness of audience delivery (reach, impressions, and CPM)
- Effectiveness of marketing at retail in increasing sales

The group anticipated that it would generate benefits for all industry participants by creating a platform for more informed decision making so that the medium would be properly valued and fully integrated into media planning, forecasting, and tracking. With this full integration into the marketing plan, further information would be gathered and shared to continually improve future programs.

Phase One—POPAI's Channel Studies

The first phase of the research involved measuring shopper behavior in different key classes of trade. These efforts began with a systematic study of supermarkets.

Supermarket Study

Sales results tracked against type of display

POPAI's pilot proved that it was possible to capture meaningful data at retail. POPAI then expanded its work to develop a base of knowledge for key channels of distribution. The research strategy was to focus on major distribution channels to expand and refine the methodology; to extract general learning that could assist all retail marketing participants; and to generate specific insights for study sponsors. Working with the study sponsors and major research organizations, POPAI undertook studies in supermarkets, pharmacies, and convenience stores.

The supermarket study was designed to establish precisely what was in each retail location and to track sales results over time for all brands and categories participating in the study. The retail audit portion of the program provided an accurate proof of placement measure and a catalog of the amount and type of marketing at retail material present in test stores; the second phase would then measure the impact of different types of marketing at retail on sales lift. In this study, retail marketing measurement was restricted to activity tied to product in the stores and did not include in-store networks or display activity supporting media messages for nonretail products or events.

The initial research was conducted during three 20-week test waves: from May through October 2000, August through December 2000, and October 2000 through February 2001. The study covered 250 retail locations including the top 15 chains, 30 strong regional competitors, and 10 independent retailers. The research was conducted by Prime Consulting Group and brand sponsors included Anheuser-Busch, Frito-Lay, Pepsi, Pfizer, Procter & Gamble, and Ralston-Purina so that data was captured for 90 brands in eight different categories. The study tracked activity at the UPC level for the categories of beer, salty snacks, cereal, upper respiratory care, dog food, carbonated beverages, hair care, and laundry. Specific data and insights related to their areas of participation were shared with the retail participants and program sponsors and a base of general knowledge was developed to be shared with the general marketing-at-retail community.

The study first established what was present within the store, defining the marketing materials measured and their specific location. Measurement was segmented against main shelf activity and free-standing displays. On the main shelf the researchers tracked the type of retail marketing present whereas, for free-standing units, the researchers also established where the display was positioned, the type of signage involved, and the form the marketing material took. Retail presence was tracked at the UPC level for all items within the brand, so that if the report indicates that a brand had retail marketing presence 25 percent of the time, it means that researchers found retail marketing support for at least one UPC for the brand during the reporting period (see Figure 2.1).[2]

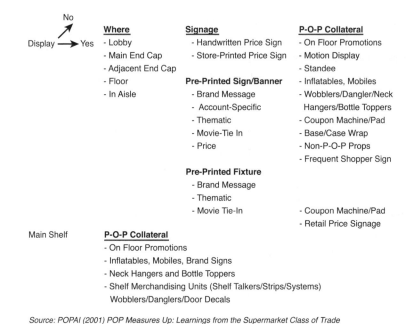

Source: POPAI (2001) POP Measures Up: Learnings from the Supermarket Class of Trade

Figure 2.1 Marketing Material Matrix

The study involved more than 500,000 observations in store to catego-
rize more than 130,000 marketing expressions tied to product sold in
the retail locations. Analysts identified 78,058 out-of-main-category displays. Of these, 91.7% were supported with signage and 25.2% included
collateral marketing material. In line, 12.7% of the 441,218 products
measured offered some level of marketing support, totaling 56,036
unique iterations of brand marketing support (see Figure 2.2).[3]

Having a full audit of all material in the store, researchers turned their
attention to the effect retail marketing had on sales results. Scan data
and audit data were matched at the UPC level before statistical models
were developed. The models incorporated current and historical factors
influencing product movement including promotion, seasonality, and
so on. Modeled results were then consolidated to the brand and category levels to produce the average results for each brand and category.
Presence was defined as any marketing activity for any UPC within the
brand; that is, if Brand A reports 35 percent coverage, it means that 35
percent of the time retail marketing support was present for at least one
UPC for Brand A during the specified period. The sales effectiveness

results capture the average sales increase or lift for the product group associated with the technique measured. By mapping the marketing activity over a wide range of stores in multiple geographies and three different time periods, the team measured the impact on sales and isolated key variables that drove results across broad categories of goods. This data was mined even further to provide specific learnings and insight to category sponsors.

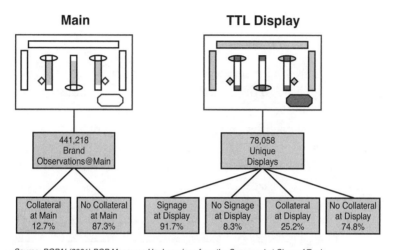

Source: POPAI (2001) POP Measures Up: Learnings from the Supermarket Class of Trade

Figure 2.2 Marketing Material Observation Breakout

Learning One: Retail Marketing Works

The key questions are, what does marketing at retail activity deliver, and how can results be improved? The data shows that, in general, marketing at retail works, but that results vary widely depending on category and execution. In total, marketing at retail material was present 27 percent of the time and delivered incremental sales lift greater than 1%, exclusively tied to retail marketing, for 41 percent of the messages in store.[4]

100 items $\longrightarrow$ 27 retail executions $\longrightarrow$ 41% success

As with multiple areas of the research results, the variance between and within categories was substantial. Main-shelf campaigns varied from a

23% to 70% success rate; outpost efforts generated results ranging from 37% to 67% (see Figure 2.3).[5]

% of Brands with a Sales Lift >+1% with M@R

	Beer	Snacks	Cereal	Upper Resp	Dog Food	Carb Bev	Hair Care	Laundry	Total
Main Aisle	68	41	23	42	54	36	70	67	49
Outpost	59	30	7	59	67	41	40	67	41

Source: POPAI (2001) POP Measures Up: Learnings from the Supermarket Class of Trade

Figure 2.3 Increase Recap by Category

The chart in Figure 2.4 further details the activity level and results by category for the application of one technique, shelf merchandising units at the main shelf. On average, merchandising units were present 37.5% of the time in these categories and generated a sales lift of 5.8%. However, the presence of these units ranged from 19.8% for beer to 54.3% for salty snacks, and the sales lift associated with them varied from a low of 3.8% for beer and 17.3% for laundry.[6]

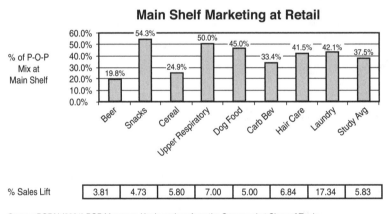

Figure 2.4 Main Shelf Retail Marketing Increases

Plotting the figures on a graph in Figure 2.5 yields an illuminating pictogram. In this case, the x axis represents out-of-aisle presentations; the y-axis is the presence of material at the main shelf. A horizontal line is drawn at 49% representing the study average for sale lifts above 1% for main-shelf campaigns and a vertical line at 41%—the average for outpost programs. Each category is then located according to its performance in each location, so that categories in the upper right were strong in both and those in the lower right were weak performers in each area. As observed throughout the research study, individual brands' performance varied significantly from these category averages.[7]

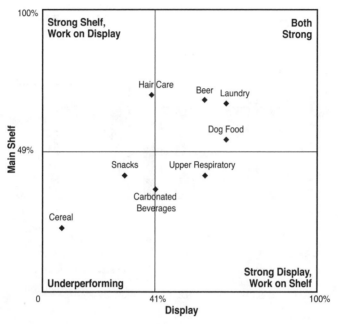

Source: POPAI (2001) POP Measures Up: Learnings from the Supermarket Class of Trade

Figure 2.5 Category Responsiveness by Location

Learning Two: Wide Variation in Execution and Results

Execution varied widely across retail chains. Results differed between retail chains, across categories at the same retail location, and within the same category. For example, a technique that worked extremely well in Category A was totally ineffective in Category B. In addition, the use of identical tactics within a category yielded vastly different results; that is, in upper respiratory brand sales, increases varied from 2 percent to 19 percent for the same material. The chart in Figure 2.6 recaps the performance of dual placement displays—positioning a product in both its main location and an out-of-main aisle display—and highlights the stunning variability between accounts. The chart recaps the activity for two categories across ten retailers during the same time period. Activity in Category 1 ranges from a low of 9% to a high of 82%; in Category 2, it varies from 0% to 60%.[8]

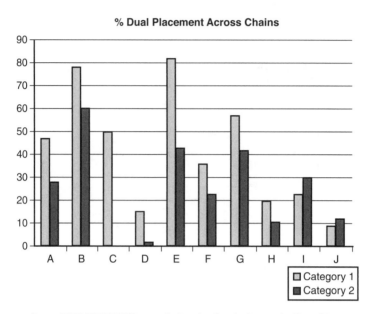

% Dual Placement Across Chains

Source: POPAI (2001) POP Measures Up: Learnings from the Supermarket Class of Trade

Figure 2.6 Responsiveness to Dual Placement Displays

Similarly, the variance in execution extends to the activity within categories, both at the same retailer and across retailers. Figure 2.7 shows that although overall category activity among these four retailers ranges from 9 percent to 30 percent, the activity within the category exhibits even more variance. Even though Retailer C has the highest overall activity for the category, support for Brand B is nonexistent. For the same brand, Retailer C delivers support at the 45% level—more than double the activity for the category as a whole.[9]

Figure 2.8 recaps the range of results recorded by type of marketing at retail treatment and location—main aisle versus outpost. For some techniques, such as main aisle coupon machines and pads or outpost danglers, the range of the recorded lift is tight, varying less than 1% between high and low. For others, such as main-shelf danglers or outpost non-POP treatments, the increases vary more than 10%. Likewise, the same technique can vary tremendously between main-shelf and out-post executions; that is, danglers generate a 4.1% to 4.9% lift in outpost displays and a 3.8% to 17% increase within the main aisle.[10]

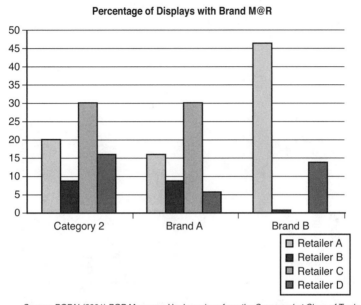

Source: POPAI (2001) POP Measures Up: Learnings from the Supermarket Class of Trade

Figure 2.7 Percentage of Displays with Brand Message

Learning Three: Some Consistent Performance Areas

Despite tremendous variability on multiple levels, three techniques consistently performed across retailers and categories: the effectiveness of shelf merchandising units, retail price promotion signage, and the impact of combining the two most effective techniques within each category. Average brand sales lifts were as high as 17% for shelf merchandising units and 10% for promotional signage. When they were combined, sales increased between 14% and 27%. However, the most effective materials differed greatly between categories, as shown in Figure 2.9.[11]

Learning Four: Consistently Inconsistent Execution

Execution was not uniform across retailers or within retailers. Although the charts in Learning Two highlight the variability in the use of marketing at retail material across accounts, researchers observed a consistent suboptimization of retail marketing programs implemented at stores.

Minimum and Maximum Lifts By Technique & Location

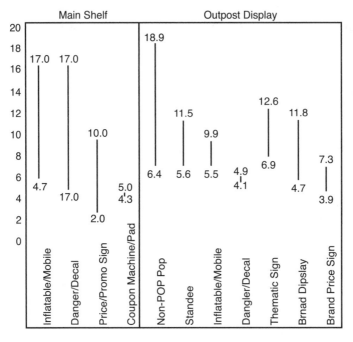

Source: POPAI (2001) POP Measures Up: Learnings from the Supermarket Class of Trade

Figure 2.8 Lift Variance by Technique and Location

Category	Combination of Best 2 Display Materials	Combo Sales Lift
A	Brand Fixture, Standee	27.1%
B	Thematic Sign, Prop	19.8%
C	Thematic Sign, Standee	19.2%
D	Account Specific, Movie Sign	18.2%
E	Brand Fixture, Frequent Shopper	14.5%
F	Any Two Messages	14.2%

Source: POPAI (2001) POP Measures Up: Learnings from the Supermarket Class of Trade

Figure 2.9 Increases from Combination of Best Techniques

This suboptimization took two forms:

- Seventy-five percent of outpost displays contained no brand messaging.

- Where messaging was present in an outpost display, the message at shelf linked to the outpost message only 13% to 37% of time.

The absence of brand messaging represents a lost opportunity to connect emotionally with the shopper and reduces the interaction with the display; the lack of coordination in messaging signals an additional optimization loss for the shoppers who visited one location and not the other (see Figure 2.10).[12]

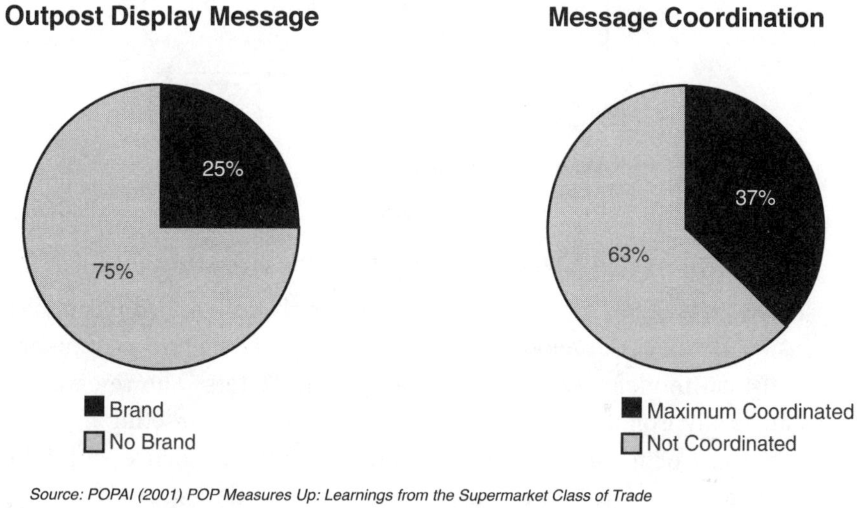

Outpost Display Message **Message Coordination**

Source: POPAI (2001) POP Measures Up: Learnings from the Supermarket Class of Trade

Figure 2.10 Message Coordination

Learning Five: Major Category Shopping Variations Within Store

The ways shoppers consummate purchases within the store vary greatly by category. Some sections, such as health and beauty aids, generate the vast majority of their purchases within their core area; other categories, such as salty snacks, rely on outpost displays for a significant portion of their volume. Generally, the variation in out-of-category purchases correlated to the nature of the product—impulse-versus-planned purchase. The responsiveness to price promotion as a tactic was also higher for impulse-versus-planned purchases. Although this observation was noted, systematic measurement of the phenomenon by category was not recorded in this study (see Figure 2.11).

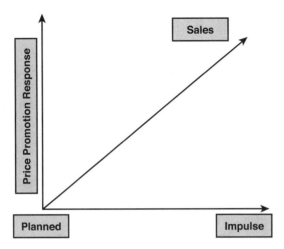

Figure 2.11 Price Savings Responsiveness

Learning Six: Accurate Measurement Possible

The impact of the marketing at retail material was assessed using sales response models developed by IRI that follow the pattern of standard statistical models used by leading brand marketers. The researchers statistically isolated the sales impact for the retail marketing material in outpost or main shelf displays to calculate the lift delivered by the material. They factored out the sales impact of other sales influencers including display location (such as endcap and feature location), price, promotion, seasonality, and so on to ensure measurement of only the retail marketing material impact. They evaluated each brand with its own response model and performed statistical tests to ensure reliability by brand. Where a sufficient number of executions for a particular technique existed, they derived lift measurements for each type of marketing at retail campaign. The research team also calculated the impact for various combinations that met the statistical modeling threshold for discrete executions in store. The average brand lift was then developed for each category by weighting brand results by volume (see Figure 2.12).[13]

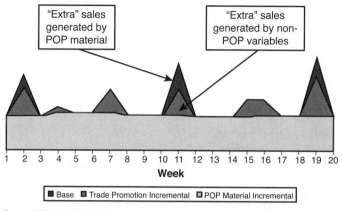

Source: POPAI (2001) POP Measures Up: Learnings from the Supermarket Class of Trade

Figure 2.12 Sales Impact

Learning Seven: Size Matters

The frequency of promotion and size of the brand promoted affected the reported results. In general, the lift percentage for marketing at retail campaigns was higher as a percentage for smaller, less frequently promoted brands and higher for large, heavily promoted items and categories. However, when evaluating the dollar return, the large, frequently promoted brands generally delivered higher absolute returns. The example in Figure 2.13 illustrates a typical example.

	Base Sales	Lift%	Incremental Sales
Brand A Infrequently Promoted	$150,000	12.0%	$18,000
Brand B Frequently Promoted	$500,000	5.5%	$27,500

Source: POPAI (2001) POP Measures Up: Learnings from the Supermarket Class of Trade

Figure 2.13 Increase Versus Volume Comparison

Learning Eight: Lack of Systematic Measurement and Learning Culture

A lack of general understanding of the sales effectiveness of retail marketing executions underlies the wide execution variance at retail. This phenomenon includes execution between stores, within stores across categories, and within categories in the same store. It also drives the inconsistent execution of branded material and the lack of coordination in messaging between locations. Although some individual participants had a strong grasp of the efficacy of a particular execution, this knowledge was not widely shared throughout their own organizations or the retail marketing planning and execution chain. Although inextricably joined in the achievement of mutual success or failure, the community lacked a formal and ongoing measurement system in which data could be shared within the retail marketing ecosystem. The extension of this lack of systematic measurement is an absence of an orientation toward shared learning that could leverage results from current programs to collectively improve future executions.

Learning Nine: Brand ROI Measurement Possible

By successfully isolating the impact of marketing at retail campaigns from other activity in the store, we can easily create simple return on investment (ROI) analyses. In Figure 2.14, we start with Brand A, which generates $2,000 in base sales per store. By executing a program with three elements (Techniques A, B, and C), the brand generates a 46.9% increase that translates into $938. Assuming a variable net profit contribution of 30%, the brand achieves $281 in incremental net profit dollars without including the cost of the retail marketing campaign. If the campaign had a cost of $100 per store, the ROI for the program would be 181% over the life of the program with a cost per sales dollar of 10.7 cents and a cost per variable profit dollar of 35.6 cents (see Figure 2.14).

Learning Ten: Significant Industry Opportunity

The final lesson drawn from the supermarket research is that the opportunity for the supermarket industry as a whole is significant. Extrapolating from the measured results, if the industry improved main aisle

Optimized M@R Mix
Simple ROI Model

Brand A Base Sales	$2,000
Sales Lift for Program (Technique A, B, & C)	46.9%
Incremental Sales	$938
Variable Profit (30%)	$281
M@R Cost	$100
Return on M@R	181%
Cost per Sales $	$0.11
Cost per Profit $	$0.36

Source: POPAI (2001) POP Measures Up: Learnings from the Supermarket Class of Trade

Figure 2.14 Simple ROI Model

execution by consistently supporting promotion activity with retail marketing material support, the increase generated would be between $350 million and $500 million. If stores added retail marketing support to the existing outpost displays, revenue would increase between $1.5 billion and $4.5 billion. Finally, if the effectiveness of the 54% of retail marketing activity that does not work is made effective through better planning and execution, we would add another $350 million to $500 million in revenue. In total the return on these improvements could generate $2.2 to $6 billion in incremental revenue. The operative assumptions in the development of this estimate follow:

- No new product display placements would be made; we would optimize only those already in place.

- Effective marketing at retail material would be placed on the shelf whenever products are displayed in an outpost location (dual placement).

- Effective marketing at retail material would be introduced where none existed on outpost displays.

- Ineffective marketing at retail programs would be remediated.

The study concluded that these results could be further enhanced through better study of the impact of messaging on sales results and adoption of a cycle of continuous learning (see Figure 2.15).[14]

	Landscape	Action	Sales Impact ($B)	
			Minimum	Maximum
Main Shelf	24% dual placement	Execute M@R support	$0.35	$0.50
Outpost	73% without M@R	Add M@R	$1.50	$4.50
	27% with M@R	Optimize technique & message	$0.35	$1.00
			$2.20	$6.00

Source: POPAI (2001) POP Measures Up: Learnings from the Supermarket Class of Trade

Figure 2.15 Sales Impact from Optimized Execution

The supermarket research program successfully applied the methodology developed in the pilot program and delivered a base of general learning about retail marketing within the supermarket channel by

- Accurately capturing retail marketing activity within the channel

- Measuring compliance and sales impact for retail marketing techniques by isolating the impact of specific elements

- Identifying basic performance drivers and capturing the variance in performance by marketing execution across brands

- Quantifying simple ROI measures on a brand basis and calculating the broad industry value of optimizing retail marketing without increasing product exposure or marketing expense

In addition to the specific insights provided to program sponsors and participants, the research also identified opportunities for the next round of research in developing a more precise audience measurement for the retail shopper audience and studying the impact of messaging variance on performance.

Endnotes

1. Doug Adams, "POP Measures Up: Learning from the Supermarket Class of Trade," Washington, D.C., POPAI (2001), page 4.

2. Ibid., 16.

3. Ibid., 19, 27.

4. Ibid., 6, 14.

5. Ibid., 6.

6. Ibid., 21.

7. Ibid., 6.

8. Ibid., 10.

9. Ibid., 9.

10. Ibid., 38.

11. Ibid., 8.

12. Ibid., 8.

13. Ibid., 17.

14. Ibid., 14.

3

Measuring Marketing at Retail in Convenience Stores

Overview

After the success of the POPAI supermarket study, the organization decided to undertake the next channel study of research in convenience stores. Learnings from the supermarket study were taken into consideration to further improve upon the research and to expand it in certain areas.

The convenience store study was completed in three phases in 2002:

- Retailer process interviews were conducted to understand the role retail marketing played within the channel and the methods used to manage and optimize implementation.

- Shopper intercepts focused on quantifying awareness and capturing recall measures.

- Store-level sales and retail marketing measurement were taken at the UPC level.

The retail audits included both outdoor and indoor advertising. As with the supermarket study, historical data was used to develop baseline sales corrected for historical events that would affect sales. The price algorithm refined in the previous studies was used to isolate the impact of retail marketing campaigns for price promotion. The R2 and ANOVA statistical tests that were used to validate the results showed stability and consistency for modeling results. The reported sales lifts do not represent the value of the exclusive use of single techniques, locations, or messages; they quantify the values of the retail marketing packages combining all three elements, with lift reported as a weighted sales average for each category.

The study was sponsored by six leading brand manufacturers: the Adams division of Pfizer, Anheuser-Busch, Dr. Pepper/7UP, Frito-Lay, Pepsi-Cola, and Quaker Oats, under the auspices of POPAI and the National Association of Convenience Stores (NACS). As with the supermarket study, Prime Consulting Group was the study consultant managing the project, performing analyses, and completing reports. Field work was completed over ten weeks in 120 stores in ten markets involving 57 products tracked in six retail chains: 7-Eleven (Albany, Dallas, Orlando), Auto Stop (Albany, Minneapolis), Chevron (Atlanta, Dallas, Los Angeles, Minneapolis), Nice 'N Easy (Albany, Dallas, Los Angeles, Orlando, Philadelphia), Sheetz (Philadelphia, Pittsburgh) Shell (Chicago, Dallas, Orlando, Phoenix).

Overall, the researchers found that retail marketing material was present 45.4% of the time, meaning that for the items studied, 45.4% of the time they were supported with retail marketing material somewhere in the store during the store study period. Figure 3.1 summarizes the number of weeks in which the brand had coverage with any marketing at retail support. The box below the bar chart details the percentage of placements in which the brand had interior and exterior support at the same time. The studied categories break into two camps: those heavily supported at retail and those with low levels of marketing at store. Alcoholic beverages and carbonated soft drinks had the highest level of marketing support—both registering levels above 50%—followed closely by salty snacks, energy/isotonic beverages, and water (35% to 40% support). On the other side of the equation, juice, health and beauty care (HBC), gum/mints, and tea collectively registered less than one-third the support of the store average. In fact, support at retail was found every day of the week for both alcoholic beverages and carbonated soft drinks, offering powerful evidence of the important role that retail marketing support plays for these categories and the category importance to this channel.

Similarly, these categories monopolized dual placements in which the category was simultaneously supported with marketing material outside and inside the store. Carbonated soft drinks dominated this execution with dual placement 81% of the time, whereas the categories of salty snacks, water, energy/isotonic drinks, and alcoholic beverages achieved execution rates between 19% and 39% (see Figure 3.1).[1]

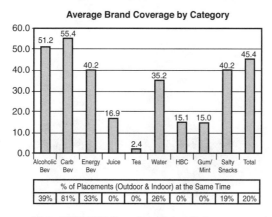

Figure 3.1 Average Coverage by Brand Category

During a typical week, the average convenience store had 25.5 pieces of retail marketing material split between 22 pieces inside the store and 3.5 pieces outside the store. In general, convenience stores had two executions in the gas area, and the others divided between the sidewalk outside the store and the parking lot perimeter. Indoor items included the store windows and core areas and outpost activity (see Figure 3.2).[2]

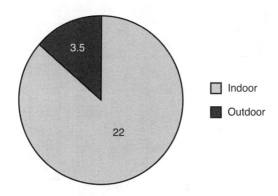

Figure 3.2 Retail Marketing Placement

One-third of all marketing occurred in the cooler section with 25% in either outpost displays or endcaps. All other locations made up the remaining 42% with food service, checkout areas, and the front window dominating the techniques used (see Figures 3.3, 3.4, and 3.5).[3]

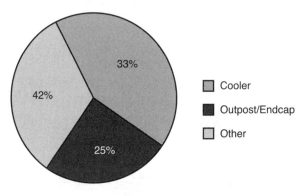

Source: POPAI (2002) Convenience Channel Study

Figure 3.3 Key Retail Marketing Locations

% M@R by Location

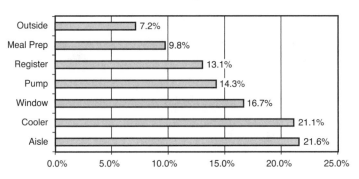

Source: POPAI (2002) Convenience Channel Study

Figure 3.4 Percentage of Retail Marketing by Location

Retail marketing generated an average sales lift of 9.2%. Lift was compared to base level everyday sales with the appropriate adjustments made for price promotion impact. Figure 3.6 compares the average percentage lift by category, with the results ranging from 2.6% for carbonated beverages to 45.5% for juice. Overall, roughly 45 percent of measured items generated a sales increase with retail marketing support, whereas

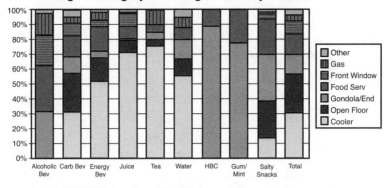

Percentage of Category Marketing at Retail by Location

Legend: Other, Gas, Front Window, Food Serv, Gondola/End, Open Floor, Cooler

Categories: Alcoholic Bev, Carb Bev, Energy Bev, Juice, Tea, Water, HBC, Gum/Mint, Salty Snacks, Total

Source: POPAI (2002) Convenience Channel Study

Figure 3.5 Percentage of Category Retail Marketing by Location

50 percent recorded no increase. For the campaigns that worked, the average increase was 20.8%. Further, observed in the supermarket study, the sales base for brands varies widely and can have a major impact on percentage measurements. The box below the bar chart details the percentage share of total store unit lift from retail marketing activity; that is, the total store unit increase is 1,000 units with 290 from alcoholic beverages, 300 from carbonated soft drinks, and so on. When measured against this standard, carbonated soft drinks and alcoholic beverages deliver 59% of the total store unit increase. In the case of carbonated beverages, the result comes from a relatively small percentage lift against a dominating base within the store. Alcoholic beverages generate their share of the total unit increase by doubling the average lift percentage in a large category. Similarly, the share of increase for teas and water is roughly even (7 percent and 6 percent, respectively), even though the percentage increase for tea is more than double the water's lift metric (see Figure 3.6).[4]

Learning One: Retail Marketing Execution Techniques Concentrated

To a much greater degree than supermarkets, the types of retail marketing are highly concentrated. The top five executions account for 84% of all material in the store, with a low of 48.4% for gum/mints and a high of 94.1% for energy/isotonic drink (see Figure 3.7).[5]

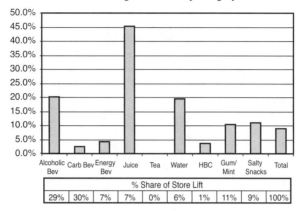

Figure 3.6 Average Brand Lift by Category

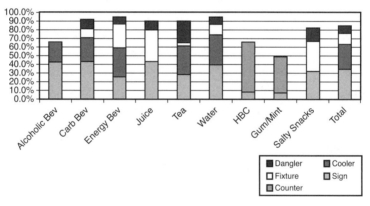

Figure 3.7 Retail Marketing Usage by Category

Learning Two: Marketing Messages Concentrated

Messages were even more highly concentrated than the type of retail marketing material used. The top five messages in relative order were brand logo, retail price, product photo, theme, and brand message. Together these accounted for 89% of all messages presented at stores, with the variance in the shopper communication ranging from 84.8%

for salty snacks and 96.6% for HBC. Product logos and price messages were used consistently by all brands but the utilization of photos, themes, and brand messages varied widely between the categories. Time in the convenience store is severely compressed, with shopping trips routinely averaging less than five minutes. Retail marketing must operate within the shopper's time and attention span constraints to be effective. Quick, efficient interactions drive results with location playing a major role (see Figure 3.8).[6]

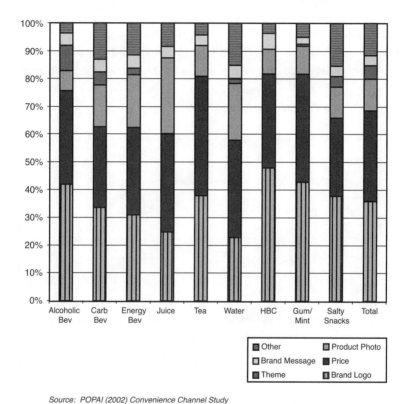

Source: POPAI (2002) Convenience Channel Study

Figure 3.8 Top Five Messages by Category

Learning Three: Huge Premium for Excellence

The premium derived from superb execution is huge. Isolating frequently used executions by category and total store results, Figure 3.9 compares three figures for each technique:

- Average sales increase for all activity

- Average lift for successful programs (removing the data for programs that had no recorded sales increase)

- Maximum lift—highest recorded increase

In total, a program that worked doubled the impact of the average program and the most successful executions often tripled or quadrupled typical results. Signs/banners, and cooler door signs were the most commonly used implementations of retail marketing (~60% of all expressions). Even with their frequent use, the positive lift was 18 percent, with the greatest increases ranging from 60 to 70 percent. Likewise, a seemingly straightforward technique, like a dangler, can generate widely divergent outcomes: 2.3% on average, but 19.1% when it works, and a peak of 35 percent (refer to Figure 3.9).[7]

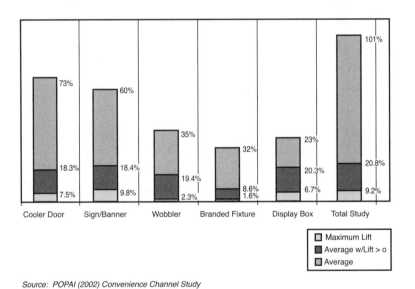

Source: POPAI (2002) Convenience Channel Study

Figure 3.9 Range of Sales Lift

Learning Four: Brand Size Drives Outpost Display Activity

As you might anticipate, large brands dominated secondary locations; that is, displays in locations outside of the core placement area. Alcoholic beverages, carbonated soft drinks, and salty snacks have a commanding presence in the open floor areas (freestanding displays and endcaps), whereas HBC and gum/mints received no exposure (see Figure 3.10).[8]

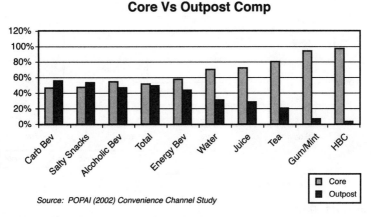

Figure 3.10   Core Area Versus Outdoor Placement

Learning Five: Category Response Varies Widely by Message Location

The convenience store heightened the focus on the role of location in driving sales results by expanding the study's focus to the area outside the store and further dissecting the location's role within the store. Some of the learning gained from this analysis includes a basic understanding of the effectiveness of outdoor locations by product type. In general, successful outdoor executions yielded strong results, with the best programs uniformly exceeding the in-store performance for the same brand. The chart in Figure 3.11 compares the lift from outdoor material against the same brand's indoor execution.[9]

Specific insights from parsing the sales results include the following:

- Gas area delivers strong results for immediate consumption products but weak returns for take-home packages.

- Sidewalk displays are effective locations for take home products.

- Small signs placed at the entrance to the store generated negligible response.

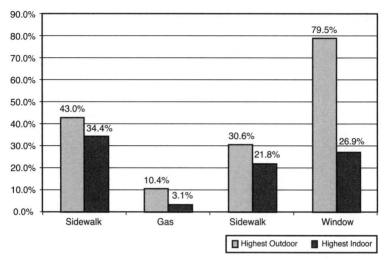

Source: POPAI (2002) Convenience Channel Study

Figure 3.11 Outdoor Versus Indoor Lift

- Advertising without product was not beneficial at the food service area. For example, salty snack advertising with product display was very successful; gum/mint advertising without product was not.

- Checkout consistently delivered strong results for impulse items with results typically in the 30% range.

- On-shelf advertising results varied with some categories generating no response and others, such as salty snacks, developing effective campaigns.

Learning Six: Borrowed Interest Has a Disproportionate Impact on Smaller Brands

With larger brands dominating secondary locations, medium and smaller bands generated results with creative expressions in their core areas and by borrowing interest. Whenever a smaller brand was linked with a dominant brand, the sales impact was significant with sales increase averaging 86%—more than five times the lift from stand-alone efforts (see Figure 3.12).[10]

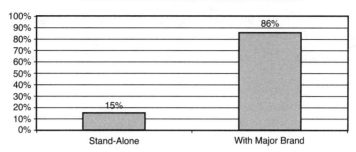

Small Brand Relative Sales Increase

Stand-Alone: 15%
With Major Brand: 86%

Source: POPAI (2002) Convenience Channel Study

Figure 3.12 Small Brand Relative Sales Increase

Learning Seven: Strong Brand Expression Significantly Outperforms Generic Treatment

Retail marketing programs that relied on generic retailer programs or focused on linking with, or identifying, a specific retailer were not effective as compared with the lift generated by custom material that had strong brand identification. Brand programs usually relied on strong imagery with high-quality production values. The study compared a large brand's custom execution within the alcoholic beverage category with the generic program executed by its smaller competitor. Across all retail marketing executions, with the exception of product photos, the custom approach outperformed the generic execution, doubling or tripling sales. Because the large brand operated from a significantly higher base, dollar volume increases were four to seven times greater (see Figure 3.13).[11]

Learning Eight: Store Is Not Overloaded with Retail Marketing Material

The research team assessed shoppers' views on the amount of retail marketing material presented through intercept interviews. The vast majority of shoppers are satisfied with the amount of retail marketing present within convenience stores. Seventy-nine percent were satisfied or very satisfied, whereas those wanting more roughly equaled those

Percentage Sales Increase

	Sign/ Banner	Brand Logo	Retail Price	Product Photo
Custom A	31%	30%	26%	23%
Generic B	11%	11%	12%	19%

Figure 3.13 Custom Versus Generic Sales Increase

wanting less. The response clustering across chains in the study was consistent. For example, whereas 11 percent of the overall shoppers surveyed thought too much material was present, the variation between chains was only 6 to 15 percent.

Further supporting their expressed satisfaction with the level of retail marketing present, when shoppers were interviewed post-purchase, 59% said that marketing at retail was somewhat or very helpful in making their purchase decision. Additionally, unaided recall for retail marketing presentations was 40 percent, indicating a strong registration of the messages observed in store (see Figure 3.14).[12]

Shopper Rating of Amount of Store M@R		
11%	79%	10%
Too Much	Satisfied or Very Satisfied with Amount of M@R	Want More

Source: POPAI (2002) Convenience Channel Study

Figure 3.14 Shopper Rating of Amount of Retail Marketing

The study also measured sales results across retailers compared to the amount of retail material they presented to the shoppers. Despite shoppers' expressed satisfaction with the amount of material across the retailer population, sales results varied somewhat with the amount of retail marketing material present. Although the study sample is not large enough to firmly establish a causal relationship, the data suggests a sweet spot for the density of retail marketing with too few campaigns depressing results and diminishing returns for excessive levels (see Figure 3.15).[13]

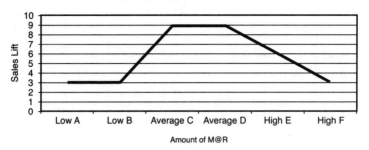

Source: POPAI (2002) Convenience Channel Study

Figure 3.15 Sales Lift for Amount of Retail Marketing

Learning Nine: Effectiveness Ratio Predicts Sales Success

To evaluate the overall message impact, Prime Consulting Group clustered marketing at retail programs into effective and ineffective campaigns based on the identification of consistently recorded performance for the combination of technique, location, and message (see Figure 3.16).[14] Routinely effective communication included product photos, retail price, brand logo/message, and savings. Conversely, generic fixtures and programs produced poor results. Effective programs included impulse products at the gas pump, take-home product at the sidewalk, beer outposts, and small-brand cooler signage. Consistently ineffective efforts included advertising without products at food service locations, signage at the front door, on-shelf advertising for gum/mints, and HBC. Stores with high-quality programs consistently generated stronger results than those with weak total programs. The correlation with strong programming is greater than with the amount of retail marketing material offered and was an accurate predictor of sales success.

A comparison of the sales results against both the amount of advertising and the level of use of effective campaigns highlights the combined effect on sales performance with the effectiveness ratio more strongly predicting success (see Figure 3.17).[15]

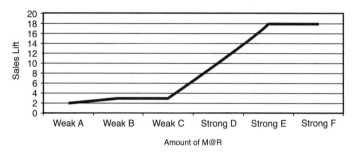

Figure 3.16 Effectiveness Ratio Impact

Analysis of Chain Results			
Chain	Amount Per Store	Quality and Mix	Sales Lift Results
A	Average	Good	Strong
B	More	Good	Average
C	Less	Poor	Weak
D	More	Poor	Weak
E	Average	Good	Strong
F	Less	Poor	Weak

Source: POPAI (2002) Convenience Channel Study

Figure 3.17 Chain Results Analysis

Learning Ten: Retailer Analysis Yields Success Implementation Model

The convenience store study expanded investigation of the marketing at retail environment to include a consideration of retailer perception of the role of retail marketing in the stores and the impact of effective management of retail marketing execution on results. The research included retailer process interviews and analyses of successful execution elements. The interviews revealed a great level of concentration on a variety of planning initiatives, such as category management and promotion planning, with less focus on executing those plans. Most organizations surveyed were now recalibrating their attention on programs that they could reasonably execute.

The evaluation of program optimization focused on the role of planning in driving successful execution and considered the perspective of brand marketers, retailers, and agencies/producers.

Effective planning includes three key areas: proof of placement, sales effectiveness, and cost efficiency. Proof of placement means simply ensuring that the intended advertising is in place where it was planned for the intended period. It is the responsibility of all participants to evaluate and improve the level of execution in store, whereas brand marketers and retailers share the burden of measuring compliance (the level of execution against preset targets) and working together to improve the accuracy and timeliness of proof of placement information (see Figure 3.18).

Proof Of Placement

Source: POPAI (2001) POP Measures Up: Learnings from the Supermarket Class of Trade

Figure 3.18 Proof of Placement[16]

Sales effectiveness focuses on the direct return on investment generated by the retail marketing programs chosen. A few of the key questions include the following: did the program work, what can we learn from this experience, and what return did the program generate? All participants share the responsibility for understanding what works and analyzing programs to develop return on investment metrics. For brand programs, brand marketers and agencies/producers would lead efforts to generate insights from previous experience, include value-added elements in the program for both retailers and shoppers, and to optimize the budget (see Figure 3.19).

Cost-efficiency measures target the maximization of the return on every dollar invested in retail marketing. The process starts with a comparison of all media options for the contemplated campaign and the integration

Sales Effectiveness

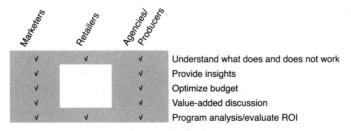

Source: POPAI (2001) POP Measures Up: Learnings from the Supermarket Class of Trade

Figure 3.19 Sales Effectiveness[17]

of retail marketing into the planning mix to both ensure that it is considered as a media alternative and that we generate the maximum return on our marketing investment by coordinating our message across all the media chosen. Brand marketers lead the consideration of available media options and integration. In this category all participants share the responsibility for planning, measuring, executing, and analyzing programs (see Figure 3.20).

Cost Effective Audience Measures

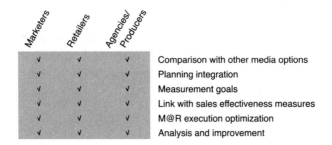

Source: POPAI (2001) POP Measures Up: Learnings from the Supermarket Class of Trade

Figure 3.20 Cost Effective Audience Measures[18]

Any program's results are constrained by the level of implementation achieved at the store. The convenience store study focused significant attention on measuring the relative success level of the retail participants in implementing the programs they planned and then dissecting and analyzing the critical success elements for the most effective retailers.

The analysis identified four key elements that drove consistent success: knowing what works, communicating the plan, commitment to executing the plan, and rewarding implementation. Although everyone shares the responsibility for implementing successful programs (just as they share the rewards), the level of involvement in each of these areas varies. Although the process appears straightforward, implementation varied widely across retailers. The chart in Figure 3.21 summarizes the importance of each success element to each segment of the retail marketing community.[19]

	Retailer	Brand	Agency/ Producer
Organizational Commitment	Primary	Primary	Support
Knowing What Works		Needed By All	
Communicating Plan	Primary	Primary - DSD Secondary - Whse	Support
Reward Results		Needed By All	

Source: POPAI (2002) Convenience Channel Study

Figure 3.21 Success Element Importance by Segment

The study data increases the knowledge base of what works in convenience stores. One retailer in the study exemplified the four elements associated with successful implementation. This retailer utilized a formal planning tool to share the expected execution with everyone from the president to each store manager. The communication tool specified what was to be implemented in each store location with an overall plan and detailed visuals by individual area. Executives carried the document with them on every store visit and reviewed compliance and sales results with store managers. Store manager compensation included a consideration of the implementation of retail marketing programs. Not surprisingly, this retailer generated consistently superior results by setting up a feedback cycle for campaign effectiveness and then routinely implementing refined plans:

Knowledge $\longrightarrow$ Communication $\longrightarrow$ Commitment $\longrightarrow$ Reward

The convenience store study built on the previous research efforts to provide additional consideration of the role of message in concert with, and separate from, location, while also expanding the research to include a measurement of shopper attitudes and the role key participants play in implementing successful retail marketing campaigns. Unlike supermarkets, convenience stores represent a fairly homogeneous retail environment with general similarities in the products presented, overall footprint, the shopper need-state, and the amount of time spent in store. The similarities across stores within a chain and retail chains within the channel facilitated the isolation of key success variables. Shopper surveys combined with analysis of retail results identified a general satisfaction with the amount of marketing material presented at retail and an indication of a sweet spot for the density of merchandising. Retailer surveys led to the identification of the critical path for executing successful retail marketing programs for store operators and the responsibilities each segment of the marketing community bears in achieving mutual success.

Endnotes

1. Doug Adams, "POPAI Convenience Channel Study," Washington, D.C., POPAI (2002), page 6.
2. Ibid., 6.
3. Ibid., 6.
4. Ibid., 11.
5. Ibid., 7.
6. Ibid., 8.
7. Ibid., 12.
8. Ibid., 7.
9. Ibid., 18.
10. Ibid., 21.
11. Ibid., 13.
12. Ibid., 14.
13. Ibid., 14.
14. Ibid., 14.

15. Ibid., 14.

16. Doug Adams, "POP Measures Up: Learning from the Supermarket Class of Trade," Washington, D.C., POPAI (2001), page 11.

17. Ibid.

18. Ibid.

19. Doug Adams, "POPAI Convenience Channel Study," Washington, D.C., POPAI (2002), page 17.

4

Measuring Marketing at Retail in Drug Stores

Overview

With the knowledge gained from previous studies, POPAI undertook its next major channel research, "Measuring At–Retail Advertising Effectiveness in Chain Drug Stores." The research team expanded its focus to build the knowledge base by more intensely studying the impact of message on shopper response and exploring the potential application of radio frequency identification technology (RFID) to retail marketing campaigns. The study was completed in two phases in 2004, with the first phase focused on developing shopper insight and the second phase centered on measuring presence and sales effectiveness. In the first phase, shopper surveys were conducted; in the second, store audits were completed using both manual and RFID tracking. Scan data was collected for the test period, and the data was merged with historical sales information for analyses and reporting. The sales and presence analyses were then merged with the shopper surveys to develop a richer level of insight that built on the previous studies.

The study was conducted in 127 stores located in 12 of the top 50 markets for four leading drug chains: Brooks, CVS, Rite Aid, and Walgreens. Following is the market breakout by chain: Brooks (Boston, Providence); CVS (Atlanta, Detroit, Boston, Philadelphia, Cleveland); Rite Aid (Boston, Los Angeles, Cleveland, Philadelphia, Detroit, Seattle); Walgreens (Boston, San Antonio, Philadelphia, Orlando, Seattle, Phoenix, Tampa Bay).

The study encompassed nine categories with four groups in health and beauty aids (over-the-counter medication, facial care, teeth whitening, and vitamins) and five in grocery (carbonated beverages, gum, nonchocolate candy, milk, and salty snacks). The research was directed by POPAI and the National Association of Chain Drug Stores. It was conducted by Prime Consulting Group with RFID measurement support from Goliath Solutions. The program was sponsored by Frito-Lay, Cadbury Adams, PharmaVite, Rand Display, Dr. Pepper/7Up, and Unilever. Store audit data and sales were collected at the UPC level over 16 weeks with base line information provided by all stores for the two-year period prior to the audit. As with the other studies, the baseline information included all current and historical factors influencing product movement including promotion, seasonality, and so on.

In summary, the study found that 32 of the 38 brands (84%) studied generated sales increases greater than 1% directly related to retail marketing programs. The average lift across the study was 6.5% with sales increases ranging from 0 to 67 percent. Twelve of the 38 brands (31.5%) recorded increases above 20 percent. On a category basis, food and beverage outperformed health and beauty aids. Despite the strong results related to retail marketing support, marketing material was present only half the time.

Learning One: Many Key Results Consistent with Other Studies

The retail marketing executions that delivered results in the previous studies also generated increases within chain drug stores. Some of the key similarities include the following:

- Weak results for planned purchase items and consistently higher outpost effectiveness ratios for impulse brands and items.

- A generally higher sales increase percentage for promotion and advertising (although the impact decreases as the amount of planning associated with the purchase increases).

- A strong response to education efforts for planned purchases and weak impact on impulse items.

- The efficacy of combining effective retail marketing techniques especially for impulse brands and categories.

Figure 4.1 summarizes these findings.[1]

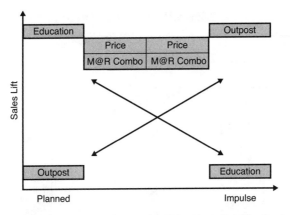

Source: POPAI (2004) Measuring At-Retail Advertising in Chain Drug Stores

Figure 4.1 Marketing Technique Effectiveness

Learning Two: Retail Marketing Effectiveness Higher in Chain Drug Stores

Retail marketing efforts had a higher success ratio in chain drug stores as compared with supermarkets and convenience stores. Collectively, marketers and brands generated a positive result 70% of time versus a 44% effectiveness ratio at supermarkets and 57% at convenience stores (see Figure 4.2).[2]

Learning Three: Message Matters

As observed in the convenience store study, the message communicated to shoppers resulted in a wide variance in sales impact. Brand photos and messages significantly outperformed generic and retailer messages; education positively affected planned purchase categories, and price was a strong motivator for both. Within the pricing category, message results ranged broadly with heavy promotional messages (rebate; buy one, get one) outperforming more generic pricing communication such as compare and save, dollar or percentage savings, and as advertised (see Figure 4.3).[3]

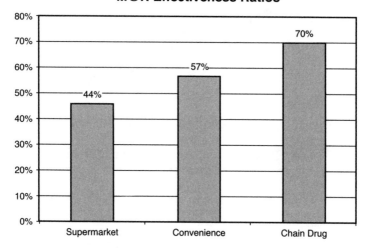

M@R Effectiveness Ratios

Source: POPAI (2004) Measuring At-Retail Advertising in Chain Drug Stores

Figure 4.2 Retail Marketing Effectiveness Ratios

Message	% with Lift
Brand/Mfg Logo	84%
Brand Message	69%
Product Photo	60%
Retailer Name/Logo	52%
Price	71%
As Advertised	65%
Sale/Save Now	68%
$/% Savings	50%
Buy 1 Get 1	88%
Category Education	88%
Brand Education	91%
New Item	57%
Rebate/Sweepstakes	100%
Compare and Save	14%

Source: POPAI (2004) Measuring At-Retail Advertising in Chain Drug Stores

Figure 4.3 Marketing Message Sales Increase

Educational executions were successful for complex, planned purchase categories such as the HBC items studied. Retail marketing programs that helped shoppers match products with their needs in categories such as vitamins, over-the-counter remedies, and facial care were successful 90 percent of the time and generated increases from 4 percent to 22 percent (see Figure 4.4).[4]

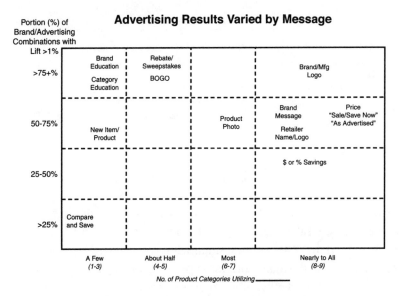

Advertising Results Varied by Message

Source: POPAI (2004) Measuring At-Retail Advertising in Chain Drug Stores

Figure 4.4 Message Impact Variance

Brand messaging delivered stronger lifts for planned purchase categories, such as HBC, than, impulse brands. Brand messages generated lifts between 28 percent and 43 percent for facial care and teeth whitening versus 3 percent to 8 percent for price messages. Conversely, brand message sales lifts were only 1 percent to 17 percent for food and beverage categories versus 15 percent to 47 percent for pricing communication (see Figure 4.5).[5]

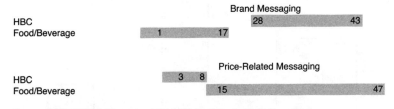

Messaging Percentage Sales Lift Range

Source: POPAI (2004) Measuring At-Retail Advertising in Chain Drug Stores

Figure 4.5 Messaging Sales Lift Range

Figure 4.6 shows the average individual category performance.[6]

Food and Beverage

Salty Snacks	42.7%	Non-Chocolate Candy	27.1%
Carbonated Beverages	21.3	Gum	19.5%
Milk	4.9%		

HBC

Teeth Whitening	6.2%	Facial Care	3.7%
Vitamins	1.0%	OTC Remedies	0.3%

Source: POPAI (2004) Measuring At-Retail Advertising in Chain Drug Stores

Figure 4.6 Category Sales Response to Price/Sales Messaging

Although milk generated a relatively low percentage increase, the dollar value of the sales increase was the highest among all the categories studied. As in the other studies, small sales bases yielded high percentage response rates with smaller brands at times recording a doubling of sales with successful marketing at retail programs.

Learning Four: Promotion/Advertising Consistently Enhances Impact

For all categories, it was better to coordinate your marketing at retail program with other promotional activity. When marketing at retail was combined with promotion, results increased from 100 percent to 1,300%, averaging a 275% increase (see Figures 4.7 through 4.11).[7]

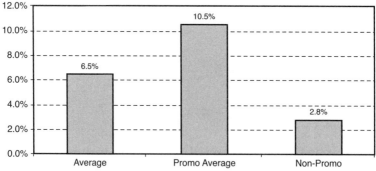

Figure 4.7 Promotion Impact

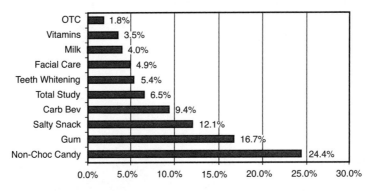

Figure 4.8 Weighted Average

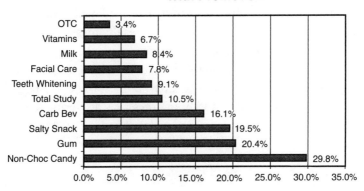

Figure 4.9 With Promotion

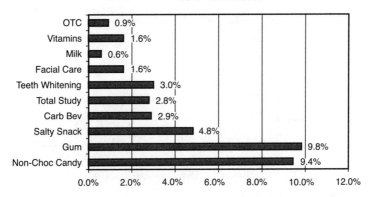

Figure 4.10 Without Promotion

Category	Weighted Average	With Promotion	No Promotion	% Change
Non-Choc Candy	24.4%	29.8%	9.4%	217%
Gum	16.7%	20.4%	9.8%	108%
Salty Snack	12.1%	19.5%	4.8%	306%
Carb Bev	9.4%	16.1%	2.9%	455%
Total Study	6.5%	10.5%	2.8%	275%
Teeth Whitener	5.4%	9.1%	3.0%	203%
Facial Care	4.9%	7.8%	1.6%	388%
Milk	4.0%	8.4%	0.6%	1300%
Vitamins	3.5%	6.7%	1.6%	319%
OTC Remedies	1.8%	3.4%	0.9%	278%

Source: POPAI (2004) Measuring At-Retail Advertising in Chain Drug Stores

Figure 4.11 Average Brand Sales Lift

Learning Five: Brand-Focused Messages More Effective

Brand-focused messages consistently outperformed retailer identification on retail marketing material, with retailer results measuring 25.7 percent below the store average. Success for retailer identification programs tracked closely with brand size so that smaller brands recorded higher lifts than larger brands. In general, the hierarchy of messages corresponded to the other studies, with photos and brand messages delivering the highest results, followed by promotion and price (see Figure 4.12).[8]

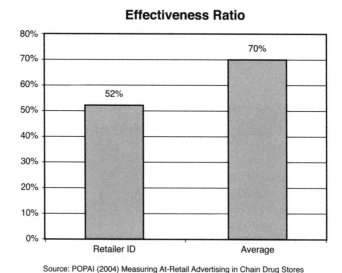

Source: POPAI (2004) Measuring At-Retail Advertising in Chain Drug Stores

Figure 4.12 Effectiveness Ratio

In total, brand messages indexed at twice the performance of programs that utilized retailer identification only (see Figure 4.13).

Comparative Lift Index

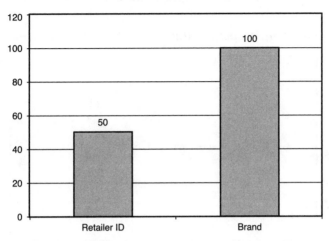

Source: POPAI (2004) Measuring At-Retail Advertising in Chain Drug Stores

Figure 4.13 Comparative Lift Index

This differential was recorded for both stand-alone programs and those integrated with promotion—the added element that routinely added the largest lift to retail marketing programs (see Figure 4.14).[9]

Promotion Impact of Retailer Versus Brand Programs

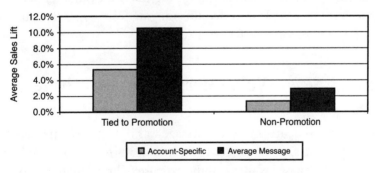

Source: POPAI (2004) Measuring At-Retail Advertising in Chain Drug Stores

Figure 4.14 Promotion Impact on Brand Versus Retailer Programs

Learning Six: Price Savings Drive Impulse Results

All pricing messages positively affected sales. However, shoppers' response varied with the specific execution, so that buy-one-get-one-free messages rated the highest and compare and save the lowest (see Figure 4.15).[10]

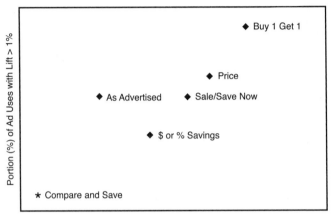

Consumers Respond to Price and Sale-Related Messaging

Source: POPAI (2004) Measuring At-Retail Advertising in Chain Drug Stores

Figure 4.15 Consumers Respond to Price and Sales-Related Messaging

Although all brands benefited from price promotion, impulse brands saw a much greater lift versus planned purchase categories. Planned purchase brands registered an average increase of less than 5 percent, whereas impulse brands recorded lifts ranging from 19.5% for gum to 42.7% for salty snacks (see Figure 4.16).[11]

Learning Seven: Value Message Drives Private Label

Although the compare-and-save message was not a strong message for branded products, it was effective for retailer private label products, raising sales for these products, at the expense of branded items, six out of seven times (see Figure 4.17).[12]

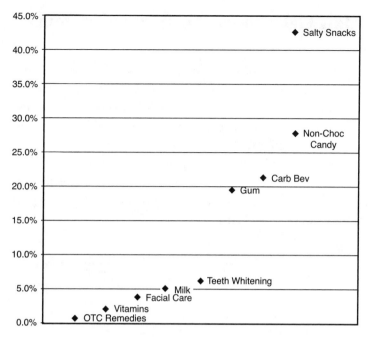

Source: POPAI (2004) Measuring At-Retail Advertising in Chain Drug Stores

Figure 4.16 Consumer Response

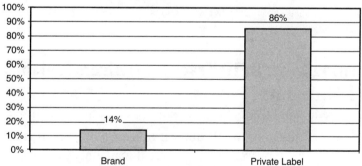

Source: POPAI (2004) Measuring At-Retail Advertising in Chain Drug Stores

Figure 4.17 Compare and Save Effectiveness Ratios

Learning Eight: Shopper Actions Differ from Words

What shoppers say and what they do vary in significant ways. In general, shoppers say that they make their decisions in a logical manner, and shopper interviews generated a hierarchy of preferred retail marketing executions, with promotions and savings at the top, followed by benefits/execution, and ending with brand pictures and logos. In fact, actions were driven by a combination of logical and emotional triggers. As previously discussed, educational triggers work much better for planned purchases, whereas price and brand photos and messages are powerful for impulse brands (see Figure 4.18).[13]

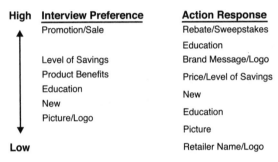

Source: POPAI (2004) Measuring At-Retail Advertising in Chain Drug Stores

Figure 4.18 Consumer Interview Versus Actions

Learning Nine: RFID Tracking Delivers Reliable, Real-Time Data

At one retail chain, RFID measured display compliance with Goliath Solutions providing technical support. In a sampling of stores within the chain, small chips were affixed to retail marketing material. A hub was placed in the store (generally in a closet or the ceiling). The hub captured data from the chips, enabling the chain to precisely identify not only whether the material was in the store, but also its precise placement location. This data was then transmitted to a central location for collection, analysis, and action. All data collection and transmission occurred without the involvement of any store personnel when the system was in place (see Figure 4.19).[14]

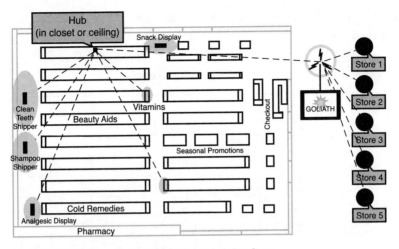

Source: POPAI (2004) Measuring At-Retail Advertising in Chain Drug Stores

Figure 4.19 RFID Typical Placement

The use of RFID enabled the chain to measure the placement of media and the length of time the retail marketing program was in use. The real-time reporting to headquarters enabled analysts to measure compliance against sales performance and communicate in real time with individual stores to remediate noncompliant situations. The daily placement and sales data were shared with managers within the retailer and participating brands to provide a more robust level of data analysis that could lead to the development of more effective future programs.

Learning Ten: Retail Audience and CPM Very Attractive

Measurement tools for determining the size of the retail audience were developed during the supermarket study and applied to all subsequent channel studies. The methodology included tracking both transaction counts and shopper trip frequency per week. The research team used this data to calculate an Opportunity to See (OTS) measurement that captured the differentiated audience for each channel. For example, the average convenience store had 4,470 transactions per week. With an industry average of 1.68 shopping trips per week for convenience store customers, the weekly reach per store is 2,660 people. In total, shoppers in the United States make more than 21 billion trips to retail stores per year—111 million households take an average of 189 annual trips (see Figure 4.20).[15]

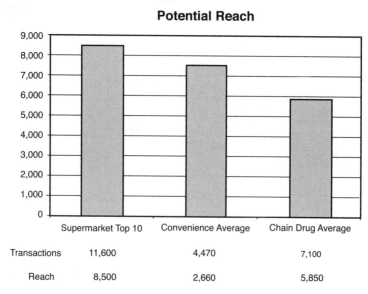

Potential Reach

	Supermarket Top 10	Convenience Average	Chain Drug Average
Transactions	11,600	4,470	7,100
Reach	8,500	2,660	5,850

Source: POPAI (2004) Measuring At-Retail Advertising in Chain Drug Stores

Figure 4.20 Potential Reach

Similarly, the cost per thousand (CPM) to reach this audience compares favorably with other media options. Although the CPM for traditional media ranges from $7 for radio to $19 for newspaper, retail costs varied from $1 for signage to $9 for dedicated fixtures. To complete these calculations, Prime Consulting Group collected costs for retail marketing programs across all channels studied. These costs included both the material and the labor required to implement the program. The analysis excluded any licensing or design costs because these are typically not included in CPM calculations for other media. Although this methodology gives us an accurate CPM measure in terms equal to traditional media, it is important to remember the positive, immediate sales impact associated with retail marketing programs. More than any other media option, the store provides an environment for cost-effective advertising and immediate sales improvement (see Figure 4.21).[16]

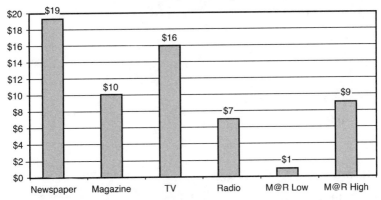

Source: POPAI (2004) Measuring At-Retail Advertising in Chain Drug Stores

Figure 4.21 Cost per 1,000 Impressions

The chain drug study built on the methodology developed and knowl-edge gained from the supermarket and convenience store studies. Although the study reaffirmed many of the basic learnings from the first two research projects, by increasing attention on the impact of message and measuring the difference between what shoppers say and what shop-pers do in-store, the chain drug study helped identify key performance drivers. RFID technology proved to be a reliable tool within test stores and provided many potentially useful benefits for mass measurement of retail execution, immediate remediation of suboptimized execution, and detailed retail marketing performance analyses. Through all three studies, retail marketing was shown to be a cost-effective medium that delivers large audiences to advertisers while also affording the additional opportunity for immediate sales lifts.

Endnotes

1. Doug Adams, "Measuring At-Retail Advertising in Chain Drug Stores: Sales Effectiveness & Presence Report," (POPAI 2004) page 16.

2. Ibid., 22.

3. Ibid., 17.

4. Ibid., 17.

5. Ibid., 23.

6. Ibid., 31.

7. Ibid., 28.

8. Ibid., 21.

9. Ibid., 29.

10. Ibid., 27.

11. Ibid., 28.

12. Ibid., 28.

13. Ibid., 25.

14. Ibid., 36.

15. Ibid., 32.

16. Ibid., 33.

5

Establishing In-Store Marketing Measures

Retail Marketing Metrics

Concurrent with the channel research studies, POPAI partnered with Prime Consulting Group and the American Research Federation (ARF) to standardize the data methods and sources to support the planning and management of retail marketing efforts. Although the general media measures are not a precise fit with the store environment, the underlying concepts of the traditional media world were adapted for the retail marketing environment so that both could be governed by the same principles, and a common language for retail marketing was adopted, consistent with the principles used in the broader advertising community. Although many of the terms in this chapter might seem rudimentary to experienced general advertising professionals, they were often new to members of the retail marketing community, who were often accomplished industry leaders but had never dealt with these concepts.

Definitions

A brief recap of the language retail marketing now shares with the general advertising world includes the following terms[1]:

- **Opportunity to See (OTS):** A single opportunity to view an ad; this is used interchangeably with exposure and impression. A shopper who passes by a marketing execution in-store, and who therefore has an opportunity to see and interact with the message presented.

- **Exposure**: One person with an OTS, also called an impression.

- **Audience**: Total potential exposures or impressions for a specified media vehicle during a defined time period.

- **Gross Rating Points (GRPs)**: Gross impressions as a percentage of the relevant population; also the sum of the rating points for a campaign or a specified portion of a campaign.

- **Target Rating Points (TRPs)**: Target audience impressions as a percentage of the relevant target population.

- **In-Store Rating Points (IRP)**: Gross in-store impressions as a percentage of the relevant population; also the sum of the rating points for a campaign or a specified portion of a campaign in-store.

- **Reach**: Net percentage of target population with an opportunity to see for a given period of time.

- **Frequency**: Number of times a message is delivered to a target in a specified period of time, expressed as an average.

- **Cost per Thousand (CPM)**: Cost of a vehicle or campaign divided by the total impressions, in thousands.

- **Recency Theory**: Advertising effectiveness increases as it gets closer to the purchase occasion.

- **Accumulation rules for weekly or average weekly media measures:**

  - Impressions are additive across stores, chains, geographies, and time.

  - Weekly Reach is not an additive. Duplications must be "netted out" or unduplicated. Reach can be weight-averaged.

  - Potential Weekly Reach is the maximum reach achievable, assuming 100% store penetration.

  - Actual Weekly Reach is potential reach adjusted to reflect the actual store penetration achieved, often referred to as proof of performance.

Potential Reach

Consider an illustrative example from the supermarket study:[2]

		Chain A	Chain B
Unique household trips	(Average/store/week)	5,437	8,161
Times	Average adults per transaction	1.25	1.25
Equals	Total audience	6,796	10,201
Divided by	Estimated trips per week	1.50	1.50
Equals	Weekly potential reach per store	4,531	6,801
Times	Store count	122	160
Equals	Weekly potential chain reach	552,782	1,088,160
Divided by	Population = share of market	21.4%	42.3%

In this example, the recorded transactions per store per week were 5,437 and 8,161, respectively. The transactions were multiplied by the average number of adults per shopping trip (1.25), as observed in the store, to determine the total audience for the retail store. Traditional media models include a consideration of the number of times a consumer is exposed to a message within a defined time period. Our model uses industry averages from the Food Marketing Institute (FMI). Alternatively, frequency data can be calculated by using either household panel data or information from individual retailers; that is, loyalty cards. Our total audience is then divided by the average number of trips to this store per week (1.5) to calculate the weekly reach per store. Multiplying the result by the number of stores in each chain yields a weekly potential reach in each chain of 552,782 and 1,088,160. By comparing the weekly potential reach with the population in the market area, we can see that chain A covers 21.4% of the market, whereas chain B reaches 42.3%.

Actual Audience Reach

To determine the actual audience delivery, we need to factor in the level of in-store execution for the retail marketing that was actually delivered, as opposed to the level that was planned. During the supermarket study, Information Resources, Inc. (IRI) measured the compliance level.[3] Currently, compliance or proof of performance must be measured by an outside service that would physically visit a panel of stores to build measurement data. As shown in the chain drug store study, RFID offers an exciting option for both increasing the breadth and depth of coverage while improving the timeliness of the information.

Continuing with our previous example, a signage program was executed in 40 percent of the stores in chain A and 50 percent of the time in chain B. Thus, the actual audience or opportunities to see were 221,113 and 435,264, respectively. It is interesting to note that in this example although chain B had 24 percent more stores, it delivered almost 2 1/2 times the audience as compared with chain A.

		Chain A	Chain B
	Weekly potential chain reach	552,782	1,088,160
Times	Audited execution %	40%	50%
Equals	Avg weekly actual reach (OTS)	221,113	435,264
	Percentage of market	8.6%	21.2%

In-Store Rating Points

Building on our frequency and reach data, we move to a consideration of rating points. Traditional media measures gross rating points (the total impressions as a percentage of the measured population for a campaign) and target rating points (target audience impressions as a percentage of the relevant population). The In-Store Rating Points (IRP) provides a unique expression for retail marketing measurement of reach percentage times frequency.[4]

Continuing with our supermarket example, chain A executes a program for two weeks and chain B executes a program for one week: 8.6 percent of the market audience shops at chain A. They visit the store an average of 1.5 times per week, so the rating points (8.6%) are multiplied by the number of visits (1.5) to generate the weekly IRPs (12.9) per week. The advertising runs for two weeks, so the total of the IRPs is 25.8 percent. Chain B covers 15 percent of the market so their coverage (15 percent) multiplied by their frequency of visit (1.5) yields a weekly IRP of 22.5 per week.

		Chain A	Chain B
	Length of placement	2 weeks	1 week
	Reach	8.6	15
Times	Frequency	1.5	1.5
Equals	Weekly IRPs	12.9	22.5
Times	Weeks	2	1
Equals	Total IRPs	25.8	22.5

Cost Per Thousand (CPM)

Cost per thousand is a common element for all media planning and is frequently used to allocate budgets across different media options and to track performance. The definition of CPM for retail marketing program is audience divided by 1,000.

	Retail marketing vehicle cost
Divided by	Audience
Divided by	1,000

The retail marketing vehicle cost includes any placement fees or labor costs for setup, but does not include licensing fees or creative expense to ensure evaluation on the same terms as traditional media vehicles. As in other examples, the audience is the number of people who have an opportunity to see the marketing campaign in the store.[5]

		Chain A	Chain B
	Total Stores	122	160
Times	Execution level	40%	50%
Equals	Stores with M@R	49	80
Times	M@R cost	$27	$15
Equals	Total Cost	$1,323	$1200
Divided by	Total Audience	442,226	436,264
Divided by	Total Audience	1,000	1,000
Equals	CPM	$2.99	$2.75

Audience Delivery Worksheet

Integrating the previous process, we can construct an audience delivery worksheet for retail marketing as follows: Weekly shoppers per store, multiplied by the number of stores in the chain, quantify the delivery of a total potential audience. This figure is divided by the target market population to define the potential market reach in-store. The potential reach is multiplied by the actual placement or execution level in-store, which yields the actual total market reach. The actual reach is multiplied by the average number of shopping trips for the retailer, and is then divided by 1,000 to calculate IRPs for the planned campaign.[6]

**Audience Delivery
Worksheet**

Weekly Store Traffic	Number of Stores		
_____ X	_____	=	_____
	Target Market Population	÷	_____
	Potential Reach		_____
	Execution Level	x	_____

**Audience Delivery
Worksheet**

Actual Market Reach	=	_____
Average Weekly Trips	x	_____
	÷	<u>1,0000</u>
IRPs	=	_____

Phase One Summary

The Phase One programs sought to systematically develop measurements for retail marketing against three objectives:

- Proof of placement

- Audience delivery cost effectiveness

- Sales impact

The thought leaders in the industry directed and underwrote substantial research to produce a methodology for measuring retail marketing activity on a broad scale while isolating the impact of retail marketing efforts from the other promotional efforts occurring in-store. POPAI, along with other associations such as the National Association of Convenience Stores (NACS) and Advertising Research Foundation (ARF), research partner Prime Consulting Group, brand marketing sponsors, and retail participants, guided the program through the pilot study, channel studies in supermarket, convenience, and chain drug stores and the development of audience measurement principles that allowed participants to employ retail marketing metrics and terminology similar to those used for traditional media.

As the research plan was implemented, methodology was defined, and a broad learning base was developed. The supermarket research established measurement principles for the retail environment and focused attention on the sales impact derived from executing different types of retail marketing campaigns; for example, a standee versus free-standing fixture. The convenience store study incorporated an added emphasis on measuring the impact of retail marketing material location (combined with type of material) on sales results and analyzed retailer execution plans against the level of chainwide implementation achieved to identify the key success elements for all participants to enhance execution. The chain drug store efforts expanded the research focus to encompass the role that message content (with material and type of advertising) had on results. To broaden the understanding of the store further, the study included shopper interviews to measure what shoppers said versus what they actually did in-store. The study also reviewed the efficacy of applying RFID technology to systematically measure proof of placement for retail marketing media.

A few of the broad-scale results include a finding on the relative use of retail marketing material by channel. Supermarkets had marketing support 27 percent of the time, followed by convenience stores at 45 percent, and chain drug stores at 50 percent (see Figure 5.1).[7]

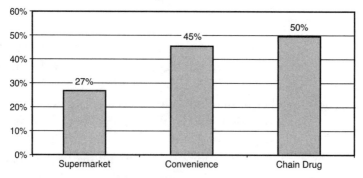

Source: POPAI (2004) Measuring At-Retail Advertising in Chain Drug Stores

Figure 5.1 Retail Marketing Presence

The retail marketing effectiveness ratio (the percentage of efforts that generated sales lifts greater than 1 percent) followed a similar trajectory with supermarkets at 45 percent, followed by convenience stores at 57 percent and chain drug stores at 70 percent (see Figure 5.2).[8]

Although chain drug stores led all channels in execution levels and effectiveness ratio, the average lift from marketing campaigns was 6.5 percent versus 9.2 percent at convenience stores and 4.5 percent at supermarkets (see Figure 5.3).[9]

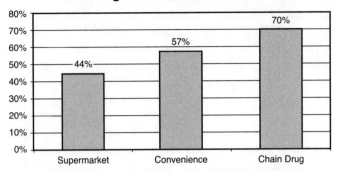

Source: POPAI (2004) Measuring At-Retail Advertising in Chain Drug Stores

Figure 5.2 Retail Marketing Effectiveness Ratio

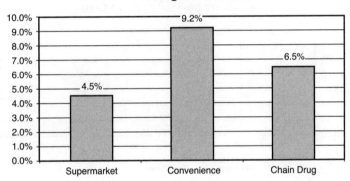

Source: POPAI (2004) Measuring At-Retail Advertising in Chain Drug Stores

Figure 5.3 Average Sales Lift

In all channels, the potential audience is huge, with major chains routinely delivering tens of millions of impressions per week (see Figure 5.4).[10]

For all retailers, the potential returns from implementing a successful retail marketing program are enormous. Average transaction sizes range from $3.47 at convenience stores to $29.91 at supermarkets. If one more item was added to the shopping cart of existing shoppers, the impact would meaningfully influence retail results (see Figure 5.5).

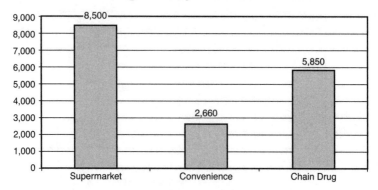

Source: POPAI (2004) Measuring At-Retail Advertising in Chain Drug Stores

Figure 5.4 Average Weekly Audience Per Store

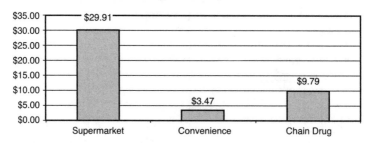

Source: POPAI (2004) Measuring At-Retail Advertising in Chain Drug Stores

Figure 5.5 Average Transaction Size

To illustrate the financial impact of adding an incremental item to the shopping basket, let's briefly consider a hypothetical extrapolation for one retailer. If Safeway achieved the industry standard for average transaction size, it executed 1.4 billion transactions to achieve its $44.1 billion in 2008 revenue.[11] With an average gross margin of 28.34 percent,[12] adding just $1 to the average shopping trip would add $417 million gross profit. Analyzing this from another perspective, an additional dollar per shopping trip has the same financial impact as an additional 49.2 million average customer shopping visits. With a modest flow through of the increased margin dollars, net profits could be improved by 20 percent.

Collectively, we have an incredible opportunity to dramatically improve financial performance by increasing the effectiveness of what is already in the store. The return on these efforts can have a profound impact on both the top and bottom lines.

Phase Two—Nielsen's PRISM Project
Developing broad-scale audience measures

Overview
Phase One research was broadly focused on three big ideas:

- Establishing a framework for the measurement and consideration of retail marketing

- As a medium that could be integrated into formal media planning tools used by all participants

- Building a general knowledge base of the key dynamics within the retail marketing environment by exploring a variety of aspects within deep channel studies

By contrast, Phase Two research attacked a single big challenge in working to develop a methodology for syndicated audience delivery measures (In-Store Rating Points, or IRPs) across multiple channels. Rather than focusing on the general traffic count for the entire store, the goal was to more accurately measure the traffic by area within the store. The model for impressions within each aisle was

In-store traffic by location

×

Compliance (level of execution)

×

Unduplicated impressions

=

IRP

The project was titled PRISM, for "Pioneering Research for an In-Store Metric," with the goals of measuring retail marketing reach by retail department and linking aisle impressions to sales conversion, to help participants better integrate retail marketing into their planning models and assist them in making better use of their planned materials. The research team would collect and analyze traffic by location in the store, day and day part, media placement, media type, and shopper characteristics. As George Wishart, the Nielsen executive director who led the PRISM efforts, stated, "Our goal is to develop an industry standard that can be applied to any retail environment."[13]

The research was conducted in two studies with four stages in each study:

- Measurement of media in-store and store traffic patterns

- Analyses of collected data and cross-referencing with other information sources for demographics

- Modeling of panel data

- Model testing

Between studies, Nielsen worked to further refine the analyses and modeling based on the results to prepare for a larger scale test that would validate the efficacy of the approach employed. The goal was to develop and test a model that would enable for syndication of store traffic based on the actual ongoing measurement of a panel of retail locations.

The anticipated result would be the in-store equivalent of network television audience measurement so that practitioners would have a third-party certified audience estimate as a necessary first tool for media planning. Instead of television viewers measured with diaries or people meters, the efforts in Phase Two focused on the physical measurement of shoppers in store aisles. To achieve this measurement, Nielsen placed infrared transmitters in each aisle that registered the traffic into and out of the aisle and then transmitted the data to a central location for collection and eventual analyses. The electronic counts were verified by personnel to simultaneously test the viability of the deployment of infrared technology (see Figure 5.6).[14]

Figure 5.6 Aisle sensor

Nielsen supplemented its in-store proof-of-placement measurements and in-aisle traffic data collection with shopper demographic profiles derived by superimposing information from its HomeScan consumer panel onto the PRISM data.[15]

Stage One

The first stage of the study was led by The Nielsen Company with sponsorship from the In-Store Marketing Institute (ISMI), 3M, Coca-Cola, Kellogg's, Miller Brewing, Procter & Gamble, and the Walt Disney Company. Albertsons, Kroger, Walgreens, and Wal-Mart were the participating retailers. The first study encompassed 10 stores, (two each from Albertsons, Kroger, and Walgreens, and four from Wal-Mart) in 64 product categories over four weeks in spring 2006.

The results from stage one included[16]

- Validation of the accuracy of infrared technology—physically observed traffic aligned tightly with infrared measured shopper counts

- Ability to viably model store traffic results from panel data—the test results yielded a much higher correlation between projected traffic by department and actual traffic than anticipated pretest

- Accuracy of predictive traffic estimates using sales and other quantifiable inputs

Beyond the measured results, the research clearly pointed the way for further enhancement and enthusiasm among the study sponsors ran high, as exhibited by this statement from Bob McDonald, then chief operating officer of Procter & Gamble. "By taking this data [and] aligning it against the cost of specific physical in-store executions, we are going to be able to establish CPM—the cost per thousand to reach those shoppers in a particular category and by store. This will lay the foundations for precisely measuring return on investment for specific executions or displays by category, by retailer. You are even going to be able to establish ROI by geography—what works better in Florida than in Illinois—or even ROI by seasonality."[17]

Stage Two

In the second stage of PRISM, Nielsen and the other program sponsors worked to test a more refined model while significantly expanding the research in several important ways[18]:

- Retail participation increased to 160 stores (versus 10) and 18 retailers.

- Product categories increased from 64 to more than 200.

- Test period moved from 4 weeks to 26 weeks to better isolate seasonality.

- Focus on building greater modeling sophistication by including geography, seasonality, promotional factors, and so on.

Under The Nielsen Company's leadership, sponsors were expanded to include not only the original study sponsors (ISMI, 3M, Coca-Cola, Kellogg's, Miller Brewing, Procter & Gamble, the Walt Disney Company, Albertsons, Kroger, Walgreens, and Wal-Mart) but also brand marketers Clorox, ConAgra Foods, General Mills, Hewlett-Packard, Kraft, Mars Snackfood, Mattel, Nintendo, and Unilever; retailers A&P, Ahold USA, Hy-Vee, Meijer, Pathmark, Price Chopper, Rite Aid, Safeway, Schnucks, Sears/Kmart, Stop & Shop, Supervalu, Target, and Winn-Dixie; and agencies Catapult Marketing, Group M, Integer, MARS Advertising, OMD, and Starcom MediaVest. The trial was initiated in April 2007 with a retail base that covered 60 percent of the All Commodity Value (ACV) of the products sold in grocery, drug, and mass retailers, which was well beyond the coverage goal. Category coverage was expanded beyond the packaged goods that dominated the first study to include toys, consumer electronics, and other general merchandise. The study was conducted continuously in some test stores and "pulsed" in three- and four-week intervals in other locations (see Figure 5.7).[19]

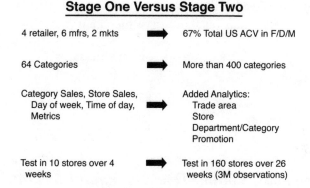

Figure 5.7 Stage One/Stage Two Scope Comparison

Research Learnings

Learning One: Modeling Is a Viable Option

The studies conclusively demonstrated that a modeling approach could generate accurate IRP metrics for both individual stores and entire retail chains while predicting traffic and unduplicated impressions by store, location in the store, day of month, and day part.[20]

Learning Two: Marketing at Retail Audience Is Huge

Building on the information gathered in the Phase One channel studies, the Phase Two PRISM efforts substantiated the size of the audience entering retail locations and also verified that they routinely traverse a great deal of the store geography. As David Calhoun, the chairman and CEO of The Nielsen Company stated, "The retail audience is enormous. It is the largest audience available today. Right now millions of shoppers are in-store. But PRISM lets us know about more than just the total audience size for a retailer. It tells us where in the store the shoppers are and how that changes by time of day and day of week."[21]

Learning Three: Shoppers Exposed to a Large Number of Marketing Stimuli In-Store

Shoppers were exposed to a tremendous number of marketing messages. The averages observed in this phase ranged from 2,300 in a typical chain drug store to more than 5,000 in a mass merchant[22]:

Channel	Average Messages
Chain Drug	2,300
Grocery	3,500
General Merchandise	5,000+

Learning Four: Volume Does Not Equate to Traffic

Category transaction data is not an accurate proxy for traffic because not all shoppers entering an aisle make a purchase from that area of the store. The learning is significant because it provides data to practitioners on closure measurements by channel, chain, and store. This data can lead to analyses to develop programs to improve the closure rate from aisle visits. Speaking about the nonpurchasing shopper in-store, Calhoun continued, "Until now, we have known a lot about the people who made purchases; however, now we have information about the shoppers who visited a category or aisle but who did not buy.... No purchase data or loyalty data can provide this insight."[23]

Learning Five: Identifiable Shopping Patterns

With its introduction of shopper demographic analyses, the study added a new component of valuable learning. Data analyses revealed discernible shopping patterns for shopper segments. For example, 13 percent of the shopping visits included children. When children were a part of the store visit, shoppers visited more sections of the store and purchased more total items than shoppers without children. The results were consistent throughout the week and across most categories. Although the presence of children increased the probability of purchasing seasonal items, snack bars, and fruit snacks, this propensity did not extend to candy.[24]

Learning Six: Differential Close Rates by Category

The percentage of shoppers who purchase a product from an aisle they visit varies broadly by category. In general, the closure rates for categories such as salty snacks, carbonated beverages, water, milk, and cookies are high, whereas rates are relatively low for mayonnaise, cereal, butter, vitamins, and eggs. In grocery stores, for example, 66 percent of shoppers who visit the aisle buy salty snacks, whereas only 13 percent of those passing the egg section actually purchase them.[25]

Learning Seven: Differential Close Rates by Channel

Just as the closure rate varies by category within the store, the percentage varies widely within the same category across different chains. For example, the closure rates in chain drug stores are generally lower than those in supermarkets. In some categories such as salty snacks, the difference can be substantial: Grocery close rate for salty snacks is 66 percent; chain drug close rate is 17 percent.[26]

Learning Eight: Consistent Shopping Patterns

Similarly, although traffic count fluctuated within a chain and across different chains and channels, the overall shopping patterns and demographics of the shopper composition showed strong similarities. Traffic counts between retailers varied, but they rose and fell during the same period and followed similar peaks and nadirs during the month. Traffic levels changed significantly during a month, but the deviations followed predictable patterns. The translation of traffic into revenue varied widely by time of day with high conversion rates in the early morning and late evening versus other day parts with higher total transaction counts, but a lower percentage of shoppers executing a purchase.[27]

Learning Nine: Outpost/Feature Location Traffic Varies
Just as the traffic into aisles throughout the store fluctuates widely, so too do the shoppers passing feature locations, such as endcaps and free-standing displays. The traffic differential between endcaps varied during the test by as much as 700 percent depending on the location in the store.[28]

Learning Ten: Store Design Influences Traffic Patterns
The store layout influenced the traffic pattern for the entire store. For example, across all channels, the endcap closest to the primary entrance (generally the rightmost aisle) is the most effective and registers the highest traffic counts; a narrow upfront area often drove shoppers to the rear perimeter, decreasing the impact of the front endcaps and increasing the value of the rear displays.[29]

Summary
Although originally planned for syndicated rollout in 2009 following successful tests in 2006 and 2007, the Nielsen syndicated service has been placed on hold as a result of the constriction associated with the current economic environment. However, the studies greatly increased our existing knowledge base by expanding the areas of the marketing at retail landscape that were investigated. The Phase One studies explored specific categories within channels and the role of the following:

- Total store traffic

- Types of marketing at retail

- Marketing at retail location

- Marketing at retail messages

- Retail execution

- Shopper perceptions

- RFID capability for capturing proof-of-placement measures

Phase Two studies expanded the research to include the following:

- Development of a scalable model for broad ongoing audience measurement and potential syndication

- Traffic by location

- Closure rates

- Shopper demographics

- Variances by day of the month, day of the week, and day part

These efforts added to the growing base of knowledge of the retail marketing environment. A.G Lafley, then CEO of Procter & Gamble, summed up the thinking about the importance of continuing to grow this knowledge base when speaking to the Consumer Analyst Group of New York on February 21, 2008: "Marketing productivity is another important opportunity. P&G invests about $10 billion a year in consumer marketing. And as you know, we've been working for some time now to increase the effectiveness and the efficiency of our consumer marketing spending—and to increase the reach and the impact with consumers."

"In addition, we spend $10 billion with retailers to drive demand creation in stores. And we're confident we can improve the productivity of this investment in shopper purchase and trial with our trade customers. Consumers claim 70 percent of their final purchase decisions are made at the store shelf, but we don't know as much as we would like about how these purchase decisions are really made. So we're in the process of closing this knowledge and understanding gap."[30]

Endnotes

1. Doug Adams and Jim Spaeth, "In-Store Advertising Audience Measurement Principles," Washington, D.C., POPAI, 2003, pages 3 – 8.

2. Doug Adams, "POP Measures Up: Learnings from the Supermarket Class of Trade," Washington, D.C., POPAI (2001), page 43.

3. Ibid., 6-7.

4. Ibid., 8.

5. Ibid., 43.

6. Ibid., 10.

7. Ibid., 14; Doug Adams, "POPAI Convenience Channel Study," Washington, D.C., POPAI (2002), page 15; Doug Adams, "POPAI Measuring At-Retail Advertising in Chain Drug Stores," Washington, D.C., POPAI (2004), page 20.

8. Doug Adams, "POP Measures Up: Learnings from the Supermarket Class of Trade," Washington, D.C., POPAI (2001), page 6; Doug Adams, "POPAI Convenience Channel Study," Washington, D.C., POPAI (2002), page 15; Doug Adams, "POPAI Measuring At-Retail Advertising in Chain Drug Stores," Washington, D.C., POPAI (2004), page 22.

9. Doug Adams, "POP Measures Up: Learnings from the Supermarket Class of Trade," Washington, D.C., POPAI (2001), page 6; Doug Adams, "POPAI Convenience Channel Study," Washington, D.C., POPAI (2002), page 15; Doug Adams, "POPAI Measuring At-Retail Advertising in Chain Drug Stores," Washington, D.C., POPAI (2004), page 16.

10. Doug Adams, "POPAI Measuring At-Retail Advertising in Chain Drug Stores," Washington, D.C., POPAI (2004), page 32.

11. Safeway Annual Report (2008).

12. Ibid.

13. Peter Breen, "In-Store Marketing Institute," (December 2006) http://www.instoremarketer.org/article/nielsen-becomes-standards-bearer/5616.

14. Joseph Tarnowski, "Technology: In-store Influence Progressive Grocer," (September 1, 2008) http://www.progressivegrocer. com/progressivegrocer/content_display/in-print/current-issue/ e3i85d526d9b2781718952d7ea1040dfaf0.

15. Ibid.

16. George Wishart, *P.R.I.S.M.* (Updated June 8, 2007).

17. "In-Store Marketing Institute" (September 2007) http://www. instoremarketer.org/p-r-i-s-m-s-promise-br-pproaching-reality/6687.

18. Ibid.

19. "Nielsen In-Store" (May 2008) http://www.instoremarketer.org/article/analyzing-PRISM-data.

20. George Wishart, *P.R.I.S.M.* (Updated June 8, 2007).

21. "In-Store Marketing Institute" (September 2007) http://www. instoremarketer.org/p-r-i-s-m-s-promise-br-pproaching-reality/6687.

22. Ibid.

23. Ibid.

24. "In-Store Marketing Institute" (May 2008) http://www.instore-marketer.org/article/analyzing-PRISM-data.

25. Ibid.

26. Ibid.

27. Ibid.

28. Ibid.

29. Ibid.

30. "In-Store Marketing Institute" (February 2008) http://www. instoremarketer.org/article/lafley-prism-will-transform

6

Capturing Shopping Dynamics in Store

Overview
Background
POPAI launched the third phase of the research after engaging senior researchers from leading brand marketers, retailers, and agencies convened to establish a strategy and develop a plan for building a more robust level of understanding of retail marketing. Although the group viewed proof of placement and audience quantification as necessary components for integrating retail marketing into media planning, the group wanted to move beyond audience quantification to measure and understand the actual interaction of shoppers with marketing material and messages in stores and their sales impact. The goal was to move beyond the traditional metrics of audience, return on investment, and message effectiveness to develop new measures that included engagement and a retail marketing evaluation model. The group designated this project as the Marketing at Retail Initiative (MARI) and defined the specific objectives and work plan for testing and developing the program to execute its goals.

The working group detailed its vision in a planning document published in May 2005: "...long-term goal for driving a paradigm shift to build understanding of and a common language for the at-retail marketing space so that practitioners are able to implement an integrated, media-neutral planning approach and measure ROI on the same terms as traditional media...."[1]

In the view of the committee, the direction for MARI represented a logical progression in thought for maximizing retail space productivity by elevating cooperation among all the key constituents: "The overview of the current project proposes that previous major retail efforts to date have been focused on NCR (increasing front-of-the-store productivity) and ECR (increasing back-of-store efficiency) while this project is focused on ICR—Intelligent Consumer Response (increasing productivity in the core, middle-of-the-store, where shopper decisions are made)."[2]

$$NCR \longrightarrow ECR \longrightarrow ICR$$

The group believed that the successful implementation of the project would pay tremendous dividends for all retail participants: Retailers would optimize the productivity of their most precious fixed asset—retail space; agencies and brand marketers would gain better efficiency for their marketing expenditures by optimizing their media mix and improving their retail execution.

As MARI developed, a key goal was to supplement the audience metrics of a syndicated service by measuring the number of shoppers who actually saw marketing at retail programs and then interacted with them. The addition of these important data points would lay the foundation for the development of a best-practices model for use by all participants. In this way, MARI was not a replacement for syndication but a valuable adjunct providing access to deeper insights into the dynamics at play in retail stores:

- How many come in (Syndication and MARI)
- How many go past (Syndication and MARI)
- How many see (MARI)
- How many interact with (MARI)
- How many purchase (Syndication and MARI)

The project focused on establishing a worldwide, standardized measurement of shopper engagement so that for every item of retail marketing material presented in store, we could measure the shoppers who passed the item, saw the item, engaged with the item, and then purchased the item. The retail marketing evaluation model would take IRPs as a starting point and measure effectiveness in terms of both engagement and purchase:

$$IRP \longrightarrow Seen \longrightarrow Impact \longrightarrow Purchased$$

As a part of this execution, the project would establish a global industry standard of measurement for

- Shopper profile

- Reach

- Visibility

- Frequency

- Presence

In doing so, the project would also deliver important learning to be applied toward a best-practices model for developing effective marketing at retail campaigns while also highlighting opportunities for further exploration and development.

Market Tests

Proof-of-concept testing for MARI was completed in two phases: a December 2006 test in the United Kingdom and a spring 2007 test in the United States. The United Kingdom test covered Morrison's stores, whereas the United States test tracked four different retailers. Participants in the United Kingdom study included brand marketers Coca-Cola, Diageo, and Unilever; the United States program included Anheuser-Busch, Frito-Lay, Hershey's, McKee Foods, and Pepsi from the brand standpoint; and British Petroleum, Safeway, 7-Eleven, and Walgreens as retail participants. Research was directed by the MARI Advisory Council (MAC) led by Don Whetstone, senior director, Merchandising Research at Walgreen Company, and was conducted by Sheridan Global Consulting. Beyond the sponsored sections, data was captured for an additional 421 categories covering the entire store in each location.

Although definitions and classifications continue to evolve, marketing material was broken into 37 classifications as follows:[3]

- Board Posters—Permanent
- Branded Counter Display—Permanent
- Branded Equipment—Permanent
- Branded Shelf Equipment—Permanent
- Bus Stops/Banners/Fins—Permanent
- Case/Stack Displays—Temporary
- Ceiling Hanging Boards—Temporary
- Coupon Tear Pad/Holder—Temporary
- Digital Signage/In-Store TV—Permanent
- Dump Bin Wraps—Temporary
- Dump Bins—Permanent
- Dump Bins—Temporary
- Easel Cards—Temporary
- Floor Displays (Carousels) —Permanent
- Floor Graphics—Temporary
- Gondola end promotions—Temporary
- Gondola Header Boards—Temporary
- Inflatable/Moveable—Temporary
- Interactive Displays—Permanent
- Manufacturer Produced Signage—Permanent
- Neck Hangers/Collars—Temporary
- Pallet Displays—Temporary
- Pole Top Displays—Temporary
- Premium Displays—Permanent
- Retail Counter Equipment—Permanent
- Retailer Produced Signage—Permanent/Temporary
- Shelf Strips—Temporary

- Shelf Talkers—Temporary

- Side Kicks/Parasite Units—Temporary

- Stack Cards—Temporary

- Standees/Free-Standing Unit—Temporary

- Stand-Alone Chiller

- Trolley Advertising—Temporary

- Walk-Around Displays—Permanent

- Wall Displays—Temporary

- Window Sticker—Temporary

- Wobblers—Temporary

To gather the necessary data, Sheridan Global Consulting utilized five elements:[4]

- **A retail audit:** A precise accounting of all marketing at retail material by store location, type of execution, and message.

- **DigiTrack software:** A proprietary program used to record, measure, and analyze individual shopper behavior, including the shopper's navigation of the store, speed, areas of the store visited, and interaction with retail marketing material and messages.

- **Prescreener questionnaire:** Recruitment of 100 regular shoppers in each store and collection of detailed demographic information. This data was entered into the DigiTrack database along with other information to provide additional levels of analysis to supplement store observations.

- **PolyTrack video analysis:** The placement of fixed video cameras and networked digital video recorders. The recorded information was incorporated into the DigiTrack program database to support detailed traffic flow analyses, total store demographic summaries, and category shopping behavior.

- **ClipCam technology:** Specially designed microcameras that were supplied to shoppers as plain lens glasses or fitted to the shopper's own glasses. These ClipCams were connected to a high-resolution digital video recording system and added to the DigiTrack database to capture a detailed record of each shopper's behavior in the store including marketing material seen, interactions with marketing material, and actual purchases.

The in-store data collected included the physical fixture, shelf position, height of marketing at retail material, type of material presented, offer, and number of times the execution was repeated. In Figure 6.1, you can see that both BAKO and Campbell's Chicken and Stars soup presented no offer to the shopper and that the Dove soap offer was presented twice with identical messages and executions in the same location (see Figure 6.1).[5]

Product Cat	Fixture	Shelf	Height	M@R Type	Product	Offer
Salty Snacks	t1	4	Chest-waist	Shelf talker - temp	Chips 50gr	New
Salty Snacks	t2	4	Chest-waist	Shelf talker - temp	Chips 50gr	New
Salty Snacks	t3	4	Chest-waist	Shelf talker - temp	Chips 50gr	Save%
Salty Snacks	t4	4	Chest-waist	Shelf talker - temp	Chips 50gr	Save%
Salty Snacks	1	4	Chest-waist	Shelf talker - temp	BAKO	None
Soap	2	4	Chest-waist	Shelf talker - temp	Dove Single	Save%
Salty Snacks	3	4	Chest-waist	Shelf talker - temp	Planet 2 oz	Save%
Salty Snacks	4	0	Floor	Standee	Nokia 3G	Save%
Soup	5	4	Chest-waist	Shelf talker - temp	Chicken & Stars	None

Figure 6.1 Data Summary

The retail marketing expressions in the four retail stores totaled 14,475, and the research team analyzed 33,704 shopper journeys, representing 487,865,400 potential shopper interactions with marketing material. Data was collected on-site from a variety of sources. Local store information was collected on DigiTrack SQL servers in each store and then forwarded to a central location for analysis (see Figure 6.2).[6]

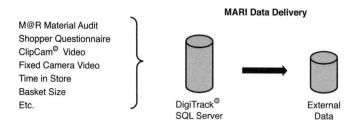

Figure 6.2 MARI Data Delivery

Study Results

The proof-of-concept tests validated the methodology used and provided a series of media metrics beyond IRPs that provide retailers, brands, producers, and agencies with tools to measure shopper engagement with retail marketing material. Together with audience delivery measures, these tools provide a basis for increasing total store productivity, tracking program performance, and improving results for future campaigns.

Three new marketing at retail metrics were developed in the course of data analyses: impact ratio, effectiveness ratio, and engagement factor.

Impact Ratio

Impact ratio expresses the correlation between the shoppers who passed the retail marketing material (those who were in a position to see the material) versus the shoppers who actually saw the material as they shopped the store:[7]

Saw/Passed = Impact Ratio

For example, if 100 shoppers passed an endcap and 50 shoppers saw the marketing at retail material, the impact ratio would be 50 percent (50 / 100 = 50%). MARI technology, along with the associated algorithms that were developed, makes it possible to calculate the impact ratios for each individual item of retail marketing by shopper characteristic and/or shopper mission.

Effectiveness Ratio

The effectiveness ratio refines the impact ratio to reflect the reach of a specific retail marketing expression against the total store audience:[8]

Saw/Size of Audience = Effectiveness Ratio

Continuing with our previous example, 500 shoppers entered the store and 50 shoppers saw the endcap marketing material, delivering an effectiveness ratio of 10 percent (50 / 500 = 10%).

Engagement Factor

The engagement factor measures the actual engagement of shoppers with the marketing at retail material presented:[9]

Engaged/Saw = Engagement Factor

If 50 people saw the endcap marketing material and 20 engaged with the material presented, the engagement factor would be 40 percent (20 / 50 = 40%). Sheridan's analyses of the data revealed a direct, measurable response to retail marketing stimuli that preceded purchase decisions when engaged shoppers ceased scanning to fixate on an object. This visual engagement was often accompanied by additional behavior including touch, pick-up, comparison to alternatives, and so on.

Shopping Equation

The MARI studies resulted in an expression of the shaping behavior within the retail shopping equation as:

$$\text{Enter} \longrightarrow \text{Pass} \longrightarrow \text{See} \longrightarrow \text{Engage} \longrightarrow \text{Purchase}$$

The definition and measurement of these interim steps enables practitioners to increase their knowledge and improve future campaigns by identifying and isolating the points at which the breakdown between potential shopper and purchase occurs.

Conversion Metrics

Using data from the MARI study, we can now analyze conversion against each step in the shopping equation so that closure can be measured against the traffic in the aisle, the number of people who saw the retail marketing material, or the audience that engaged with the presentation.

Purchased / Passed = Traffic Conversion

If 10 shoppers purchase an item against the 100 who entered the aisle, our traffic conversion is 10 percent (10 / 100 = 10%).

Purchased / Saw = Impact Conversion

Considering our conversion as a subset of the impact ratio for our retail campaign, we can track our performance as 10 purchases against the

50 shoppers who saw the campaign delivering a 20 percent conversion (10 / 50 = 20%).

Purchased / Engaged = Engagement Conversion

Finally, we can measure our ability to move from engagement to purchase by calculating the percentage of shoppers who consummated a transaction after engaging with the display. In this case, our conversion would be 50 percent (10 / 20 = 50%).

Retail Marketing Ratios

The added level of detail and precise measurement of shoppers' behavior at each step of the shopping process gives us more robust detail on our effectiveness at each critical juncture. We can now measure our performance in terms of our impact ratio, effectiveness ratio, engagement factor, and conversion. Further, we can track our performance at any level of detail for any individual element and any combination of elements, including store, location, execution, height, message, and so on.

Item Tracking

Items were recorded both by unique expression and frequency of presentation so that the study included the repetition of the same message in the same location. The following results shown in Figure 6.3, for example, that in 7-Eleven stores, virtually every presentation of retail marketing material was unique, whereas at Dominick's, 46 percent of the marketing expressions were duplicative. In total, the average frequency for repeating a message in the same location was 1.8 times. Shelf talkers were the overwhelming choice for type of execution, accounting for almost 78 percent of the retail marketing activity in the stores measured with an average frequency of 1.87 percent (see Figure 6.3).[10]

	Temporary		Permanent		Total M@R	
	Items	Quantity	Items	Quantity	Items	Quantity
7-Eleven	117	117	52	53	169	170
BP	96	109	58	59	154	168
Dominick's	4,567	8,593	451	785	5,018	9,378
Walgreens	2,396	4,140	507	619	2,903	4,759
Total	7,176	12,959	1,068	1,516	8,244	14,475

Figure 6.3 Audit Data

Examples of Retail Marketing Ratios

Sheridan Global Consulting traced the height of all retail marketing and found significant variance between the distribution of the material and its impact with shoppers. In general, the messages at waist level were the most prolific executions (59.4% of the total) and also the most effective, registering a 41.3 percent impact ratio. Conversely, overhead signage accounted for 0.4 percent of the total executions, achieving an 8.2 percent impact ratio (see Figure 6.4).[11]

Sample–POP by Height and Impact

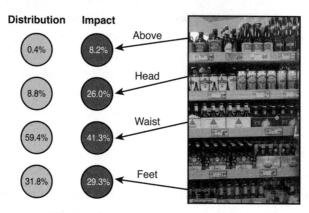

Figure 6.4 Impact by Height

Across the stores measured, retail marketing executions at waist level indexed at 114 versus 81 at foot level, 72 at eye level, and 23 above (see Figure 6.5).[12]

Location	Distribution	Impact	Index
Above	0.4%	8.2%	23
Head	8.8%	26.0%	72
Waist	59.4%	41.3%	114
Foot	31.8%	29.3%	81
Total	100.0%	36.2%	100

Figure 6.5 Height Effectiveness Index

When we first saw these results, we were somewhat taken aback. One of the retail adages from time immemorial held that you placed the things you wanted shoppers to see and buy (generally high-margin items) at eye level, and things you wanted to minimize at lower levels on the shelf. Thus, you would place tennis rackets (high margin) at eye level and tennis balls (low margin) on the base shelf. At first, these measurements seemed to conflict with this time-honored strategy.

As we analyzed the data further, we found that many retailers had executed this strategy so broadly that the key brands tended to be relegated to the lower shelves, whereas private-label products predominantly occupied higher shelves.

Shoppers were not wandering through the store in a depressed frame of mind with downward-cast eyes; they were looking for brands, and these brands also happened to support their products with more marketing material than the private-label items.

As we work through the shopper models in the next section and the tools for optimizing retail marketing programs, we expand on why this phenomenon occurs and how marketers can use this insight to their advantage.

The overall impact ratio across all stores was 16.6 percent (see Figure 6.6). Shoppers were exposed to an average of 1.5 pieces of marketing material every second they were in the store, and engaged with a display every 4.3 seconds. Floor graphics and pallet displays had the highest impact at 34 percent, whereas temporary wall displays registered the lowest impact at 1 percent.[13]

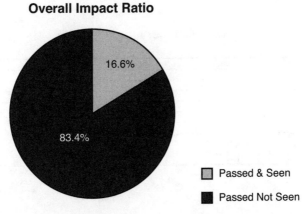

Figure 6.6 Overall Impact Ratio

With detailed classification of the material at retail and precise tracking of shopper journeys through, and interactions within, the store, we can measure all marketing at retail ratios at any desired level. In store A, shown in Figure 6.7, the overall impact ratio was 18 percent. However, permanent manufacturer-provided signage achieved a high impact ratio of 56 percent, whereas the permanent free-standing displays registered only 2 percent.[14]

Store Material Impact Ratios

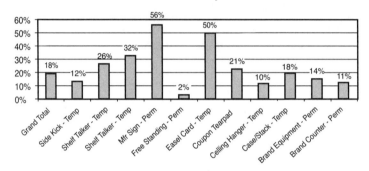

Figure 6.7 Store Material Impact Ratios

Similarly, we can break out the impact of messages for the entire store or any level of within the store desired (see Figure 6.8). In the health and beauty aids category (HBA), "Wow" was very effective (47 percent) versus a low "for percentage off of" 5 percent and a 15 percent category average.[15]

HBA Category Impact Ratio

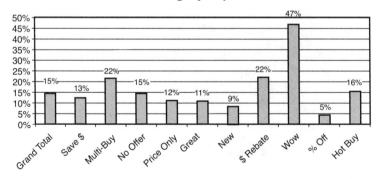

Figure 6.8 HBA Category Impact Ratio

The analyses can be continued down to the brand level where, as shown in Figure 6.9, brand A achieved the highest impact (21 percent) with a dollar savings message against a 14 percent brand average and 7 percent "New Item" ratio.[16]

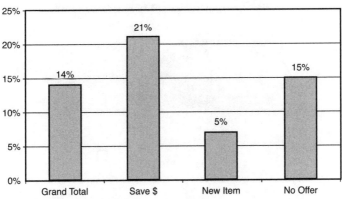

Figure 6.9 Brand A Message Impact Ratio

Continuing the analyses further, retailers can also compare brands in the same category, as shown in Figure 6.10, where performance varied significantly between brands utilizing the same type of material.[17]

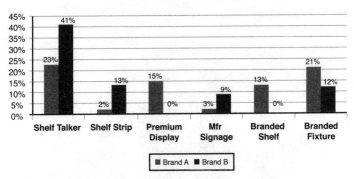

Figure 6.10 Impact Ratio Brand Comparison

Effectiveness ratios can also be tracked at multiple levels. In the stores studied, the overall effectiveness ratio was 2.7 percent. Shoppers did not visit 81.3 percent of the store aisles. Of the 18.7 percent of the aisles visited, shoppers saw 16.6 percent of the marketing material presented; that is, 18.7% ×16.6% = 2.7% (see Figure 6.11).[18]

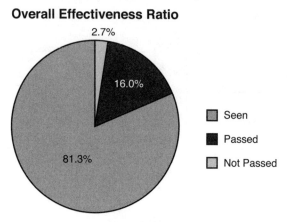

Figure 6.11 Overall Effectiveness Ratio

Likewise, we can analyze results by execution; that is, dump bins, with their location predominantly in main aisles, are passed by 86 percent of shoppers and are seen by 37 percent of those entering the store (see Figure 6.12).[19]

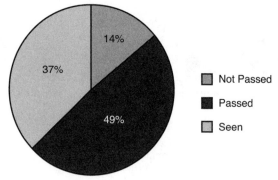

Figure 6.12 Dump Bin Effectiveness Ratio

We can also track message effectiveness with promotion or without. In Figure 6.13, a brand message, categorized as no offer, significantly outscored all other options, delivering 87 points against a next highest score of 5 percent (see Figure 6.13).[20]

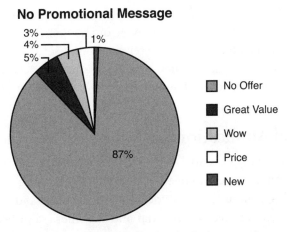

No Promotional Message

Legend:
- No Offer
- Great Value
- Wow
- Price
- New

Figure 6.13 No Promotional Message Effectiveness Ratio

When promotional messages are considered as a group, multipack offers outscored a specific dollar savings 69 percent to 27 percent, with all other messages trailing significantly (see Figure 6.14).[21]

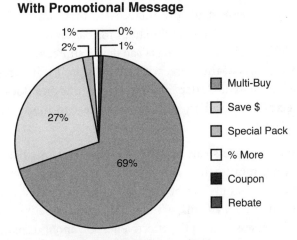

With Promotional Message

Legend:
- Multi-Buy
- Save $
- Special Pack
- % More
- Coupon
- Rebate

Figure 6.14 Effectiveness Ratio With Promotional Message

As in the PRISM Phase Two project, the generation of detailed traffic flow analyses was enormously beneficial. The knowledge of how shoppers navigate the store and which sections they visit is not generally collected or tracked and provided immediate benefit, especially to the retail participants. During the test period, 33,704 shoppers entered the store. Their individual and collective journeys were evaluated by day, day part, gender, and age. The analyses of shopper flow resulted in a traffic pattern map that showed the relative volume of shoppers for each area of the store, so that studies' participants had an accurate view of which areas were visited and how traffic flowed throughout the store.[22]

Potential Applications

MARI offers many potential benefits for all retail participants. Brand marketers can increase the effectiveness of their marketing expenditures and optimize their budgets by understanding the reach and effectiveness of each individual piece of material and the interaction between elements in an entire campaign for a store, a section, against competitors, by type of display, location of display, and message communicated. Each element can be studied separately or in concert with others. If desired, differences between day parts and within various demographic segments can be isolated and explored for tighter targeting.

In addition to the preceding brand benefits, retailers can also use the knowledge to increase space productivity in their stores, boost their operational efficiency, and build the shopping basket size. By identifying cold spots within their stores, retailers can devise strategies to move traffic through more parts of the store, with the increased traffic resulting in more items purchased. Understanding what works and does not work with the necessary specificity can allow retailers to more intelligently deploy their assets against effective programs.

Agencies and producers can reap benefits in more intelligently planning, targeting, monitoring, measuring, and refining campaigns for their clients. Sales results can be enhanced as they integrate marketing at retail into their media plans, with demographic targeting available as an option. The assessment of the effectiveness of, and interplay between, various marketing elements can enable agencies to evaluate and analyze the performance of complete programs and the components within them, so they can refine future marketing campaigns. The ongoing use of marketing at retail ratios can build the knowledge base, leading to the establishment of important client benchmarks for each stage of the shopping equation.

Most important, shoppers can reap important benefits from improvements in store layout, design, and presentation. The net result can be a store environment that offers more shopper efficiency. Together with the enhanced communication that comes from data analyses, the shopper can do less work in-store, resulting in greater shopping satisfaction.

Recap

Building on the studies completed in phases one and two, the MARI research deepened the exploration of retail marketing in important ways by

- Expanding shopper screening to include intent and demographics

- Tracking the height of each piece of retail marketing material

- Surveying the placement of each piece of marketing material to track duplicative executions

- Measuring the shopper interaction with retail marketing expressions for both seeing and engaging

- Identifying where an item was purchased as opposed to only whether an item was bought

These efforts enable us to map the path of the shopper along a shopping equation that begins with store entry and concludes with the final purchases made. The analyses of the interactions at each step in this process yields important insight into the opportunity areas in each phase. The goal of every participant in retail is to get one more item in the shopping basket. The data from MARI helps us identify how we can achieve this goal by improving our effectiveness at each step:

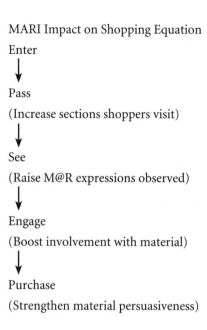

MARI Impact on Shopping Equation

Enter

Pass
(Increase sections shoppers visit)

See
(Raise M@R expressions observed)

Engage
(Boost involvement with material)

Purchase
(Strengthen material persuasiveness)

Armed with detailed knowledge of shopper behavior, our task becomes immeasurably easier. As Martin Kingdon, managing director of Sheridan Global Consulting, rightly concluded.

"If we know

- What engages the shopper

- Whom we engage

- To what degree we engage them

- Where we engage them and

- For how long they are engaged

We can make educated guesses to why and intelligently recommend actions."[23]

In addition to validating the test methodology, the MARI proof-of-concept test yielded knowledge about many other areas of the shopping experience for further exploration in the next stage of research. Some of these learnings include

- **Shopping rate**—Average speed in store

- **Shopping length**—Average time in store
- **Orientation**—Time in store until first display seen
- **Commitment**—Time to first purchase
- **Frequency**—Number of times same message is observed
- **Gender differences**
- **Traversing**—Proportion of shoppers passing through versus shopping a category
- **Mapping**—Understanding secondary and tertiary involvement with marketing at retail presentations
- **List impact**—Difference between list and memory shoppers
- **Couponing**—Effectiveness of in-store offers in changing traffic patterns

As we finalize this manuscript, the second stage of the ongoing MARI research is preparing to launch in the field.

Summary

With the constant adjustments to planning and execution that come with new ventures that provide knowledge that sometimes confounds expectations and upends the conventional wisdom, research into the world of retail marketing has significantly evolved over the 11 years of industry field research. From channel studies, through syndication pilots, to a proof-of-concept for the intense study of shopper behavior in store, the industry collectively explored all the elements that contribute to retail marketing success. Studies have been broadly directed at the dynamics within a distribution channel, tightly centered on specific measures across broad distribution, and immersively focused on shopper behavior at retail. They are all linked in growing our knowledge base, and together they provide powerful learnings while also charting a course for future development here and in other markets around the world.

Figure 6.15 depicts the focus of each of the research projects completed. MARI was deeply focused on a number of elements in a small cluster of retail locations. The channel studies explored a significant number of stores in individual channels with an ever-expanding list of activity to be measured and analyzed. PRISM concentrated on a defined set of measurements but worked to execute those measurements broadly against a multitude of channels and locations within each.

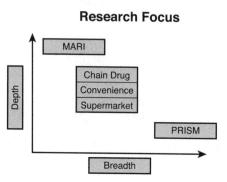

Figure 6.15 Research Focus

As valuable as the syndicated research is for expanding the base of industry knowledge, it does not obviate the need for continuing proprietary research. Although industry research provides stand-alone insights, its real power lies in its integration with the specific information and understanding gained from the research conducted by individual brands, retailers, and agencies about their specific strengths, weaknesses, and the attendant opportunities. Both industry and proprietary research provide distinctly unique areas of market intelligence. When the two are successfully combined, the result is an added depth of perspective that can enhance the strategy for the development of new opportunities and a greater level of retail success.

The Retail Marketing Model Shifts

The traditional marketing mix is under profound stress. Howard Schultz, the CEO of Starbucks, went so far as to exclaim, "Traditional marketing and brand-building have become obsolete."[24] In our new reality, successful marketers will adopt a new model that drives increased efficiency and optimizes marketing expenditures across all media options. They will use the information and enlightenment from the last decade's research initiatives to guide their planning and execution.

The shopper is now firmly in control—she is empowered to find what she wants when she wants it, and she expects to do this quickly and efficiently. The October 2007 GMA Study by Deloitte Consulting observed, "Consumer experts say about 70% of purchase decisions are made in grocery stores...what little shreds of brand loyalty and awareness consumers still have, get left behind the minute they step through that automatic door."[25] To ensure survival and success, each member of the retailing community must access and apply all the learning available from the research to date and aggressively work to expand the information available.

Today we are in the midst of a dramatic shift in retail marketing that will result in the elevation of discourse from the tactical to the strategic. Figure 6.16 demonstrates some of the major shifts that accompany the integration of retail marketing into media planning. These changes, driven by the availability of regularly provided reliable data, include the evaluation of retail campaigns against both short-term sales development and long-term brand-building.

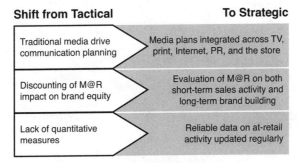

Figure 6.16 Retail Marketing Discourse Shift

These shifts imply that retail marketing becomes another option in the media arsenal, with the specific execution chosen for its applicability against the target in the selected channel, much as radio or television programming is chosen to reach a desired audience (see Figure 6.17).

The research leads us to a new best-practices model in which four key elements of retail marketing implementation are tracked across four measures. The specific marketing program is considered in terms of its

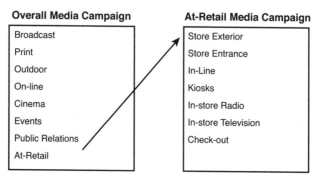

Figure 6.17 Media Integration

location in the store, the message it delivers in that location, the expression the marketing takes both in type of marketing presented and the creativity incorporated into the design, and finally the level of execution or retail placement achieved. These components of the retail program are then evaluated against the audience delivered, the impact achieved, the level of shopper engagement generated, and their closure rate (see Figure 6.18).

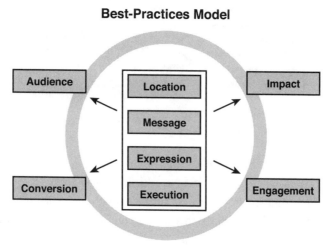

Figure 6.18 Best-Practices Model

Our new best-practices model in Figure 6.19 supports this model for retail marketing, in which the marketing insights generated from syndicated and proprietary research are incorporated into media plan development. The resulting programs are placed in-store using knowledge from previous campaigns to improve the impact of each successive placement. Each crucial step in the buying process is measured from compliance to opportunity to see (Impact), to shopper engagement (Engagement Factor), to conversion, culminating in brand loyalty and increased brand equity.[26]

Marketing-at-Retail Model

Figure 6.19 Retail Marketing Model

Endnotes

1. Author's notes (Washington DC, May 2005).

2. Ibid.

3. Martin Kingdon, MARI Measuring Shopper Engagement (Alexandria, VA: POPAI 2007), page 15.

4. Ibid., 7.

5. Ibid., 21.

6. Ibid., 3.

7. Ibid., 3.

8. Ibid., 3.

9. Ibid., 10.

10. Ibid., 22.

11. Ibid., 22.

12. Ibid., 14.

13. Ibid., 13.

14. Ibid., 14.

15. Ibid., 14.

16. Ibid., 13.

17. Ibid., 16.

18. Ibid., 17.

19. Ibid., 17.

20. Ibid., 18.

21. Ibid., 18.

22. Author's notes (January 2007).

23. Martin Kingdon, POPAI Johannesburg, South Africa Marketing at Retail Conference, September 2008.

24. Jeremy Dann, "How to Find a Hit as Big as Starbucks," Business 2.0. (May 2004) http://money.cnn.com/magazines/business2/business2_archive/2004/05/01/368250/index.htm.

25. Deloitte Consulting, "Grocery Manufacturers Association Study" (October 2007) http://www.mediapost.com/publications/?fa=Articles.printFriendly&art_aid=69231.

26. Author's notes (December 2006).

7
Shopper Models

Retail Marketing Definition

We subscribe to the definition of retail marketing as "all the activity that occurs approaching, within, and exiting retail locations."[1]

Marketing at retail takes three forms:

- Branded manufacturers branding, marketing, and selling their products at retail

- Retailers branding, marketing, and selling their private-label products in their stores

- Retailers branding and marketing their stores in the general marketplace

Brands need retailers for the distribution they provide; retailers need brands to support the statements they want to make with their store's positioning against other retail competitors and to drive category traffic. Even while brands are helping retailers with their positioning and the improvement of category results, retailers work to increase the share of private-label sales at the expense of the brands with whom they "partner."

The job of all retail marketers is to leverage conscious and subconscious shopper behavior to improve results. The macro trends affecting retail create a newly empowered shopper operating within a hypercompetitive retail environment. Winning marketers must combine an understanding of what the shopper does and why she does it to design the optimal retail solutions that deliver superior results.

Shopper Understanding

The cognitive and behavioral research on shopper behavior focuses on information processing and decision making. This research can be broken into four general groupings according to the operative behavior drivers studied:

- Cognitive

- Logical

- Social

- Biologic

Cognitive studies focus on the subconscious use of schemata we employ to help us navigate a world that would otherwise quickly overwhelm us. Logical studies concentrate on the way we apply an analytical approach to completing our shopping missions, whereas social studies focus on the role groups play in driving our shopping decisions. Biologic studies center on the hard-wired elements of the brain at work in the way we process information and make decisions as tracked through neural mapping. Because we are such complex creatures, it is our view that all four elements work in concert to influence behavior in stores.

Cognitive Research

The application of cognitive research to retail marketing begins with an acknowledgment that today's retail stores are too complex to deal with on a strictly rational level. A typical grocery store contains 30,000 SKUs supported, in the stores MARI measured, by 9,378 pieces of marketing material. If we spent just one-half second on each item or message option presented, we would be in the store for 55 hours. To deal with the complexity we face at retail and in the world in general, we need tools for simplification and improved efficiency. From an information processing standpoint, we employ selective perception and schemata to maintain our equilibrium and to operate effectively within a world that would otherwise overwhelm us. The example in Figure 7.1 illustrates some of the tools we all use to process information. It has been used to great effect by Dr. Hugh Phillips of Phillips, Foster & Boucher in Canada to describe our approach to the retail experience.

Deselection

Mark your time with a timer and then look at Figure 7.1 and stop the time when you locate the black oval:[2]

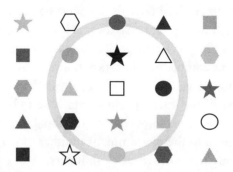

Figure 7.1 Deselection

There are 25 symbols in the illustration. If you spent even one-fourth of a second on each symbol, it would have taken you six and one-quarter seconds to complete the assigned task. If you are like most people, you were much more efficient than that because you used a shortcut to locate the black oval. You scanned the illustration in search of the desired object and stopped when you attained your goal. This behavior is analogous to our use of brands and signage to assists us in our efficient movement through a modern store.

Looking away from the figure, can you recall what symbol was to the right or left of the oval? Can you recall what was above or below? Again, unless you have Rain Man-like powers of observation and short-term memory recall, you likely can recall nothing other than the position of the oval. In addition to scanning to locate the targeted symbol, you deselected everything that did not fit the criteria. Either you did not see it, or you saw it and discarded it as irrelevant to the task at hand.

Psychologists refer to a related concept as "inattentional blindness." The concept was forcefully demonstrated by Daniel Simons and Christopher Chabris in a study they conducted in the 15th-floor elevator lobby at Harvard University.[3] They prepared videos of two teams, one dressed in white and the other dressed in black, passing a basketball back and forth. They recruited subjects and asked them to view the video and to count the number of successful passes completed by the team in white. In one version of the video, a woman dressed in a gorilla costume entered after 45 seconds and walked right through the scene. Although she is clearly visible for a full 5 seconds, 56 percent of all participants did not recall the appearance. In a second version of the tape, the costumed character stops, faces the camera, and pounds her chest before walking off. Even with this extremely disruptive behavior that lasted 9 seconds, 55 percent of the subjects did not recall the gorilla. The test subjects were so completely focused on completing their task that they screened out everything that was not relevant to that task. To break through this focus, the disruptive power of the interruption would have to be extraordinarily powerful. Compare this example of unintentional screening while processing information to the predominant number of marketing at retail executions that are never observed by shoppers.

Conscious Processing

Borrowing another example from Hugh Phillips, look at Figure 7.2 for six seconds and look away after trying to remember as many groupings as possible:[4]

ktr	ytt	oid	kde	hfgh
wqq	xcx	bnr	mnb	bnv
klb	hgp	rds	apn	iuy
ldj	wpd	zdl	ncb	oxc
ugm	tbf	jnr	ubm	rkg

Figure 7.2 Conscious Processing

Most participants can remember fewer than seven of the groupings. As Hugh Phillips notes in *The Power of Marketing at Retail*, "the capacity of the attention span is surprisingly limited. Scientists measure the capacity of the attention span in terms of chunks—a chunk being a well-known word or phrase. Under laboratory conditions, it has been found to be around seven 'chunks.' However in the real world it is less."[5]

Try the experiment again with a second set of letter groupings in Figure 7.3.

NBC	KGG	BOY	RTY
DEA	TYP	HUD	WSX
FOX	LRP	SIS	RFV
FBI	GHJ	FUN	TGB
CBS	MNB	BAD	YHN

Figure 7.3 Conscious Processing

If you were like most participants, you remembered more of the letter groupings because they were familiar to you. If you were quick and clever, perhaps you created a mnemonic scheme to help you remember more of the groupings. You might have found relations between groups such as three networks (NBC, CBS, FOX), federal government agencies (FBI, DEA, HUD), or created a story such as, "a BOY and his SIS had FUN being BAD." If you did so, you were trying to increase your efficiency (the number of things you could remember) by decreasing the number of things that you had to recall. What is almost certain is that all the groupings you retained came from columns one and three and none from columns two and four. We all screen for the groupings that had meaning. It is hard work to use our conscious attention. We subconsciously look for ways to make our lives easier and fulfill our duties more efficiently by screening, seeking things that have meaning, and looking for patterns.

Selective Perception

What we observe is not necessarily what we see. Our brains deal with only a fraction of what we "see," and we sometimes process information differently than the way it is presented. Optical illusions offer a prototypical illustration of selective image processing. In Figure 7.4, you see either a duck or a rabbit, depending on which elements you selectively process.[6]

Pattern and Structures

We use our mental capacity to identify meaning in the images we confront and establish an order in the world around us. To make this task easier, we employ an underlying organizational pattern or structure.[7]

Figure 7.4 Selective Perception

The utilization of these conceptual frameworks allows us to complete everyday tasks on a type of autopilot that does not make us work as hard and frees our conscious processing for other tasks. In the beginning, these shortcuts involve a conscious learning. Over time and through repetition, they become "second nature" and we perform these tasks automatically. Examples include any type of sporting endeavor pursued diligently over time, whether it is driving a golf ball, skiing downhill, or shooting a free throw.

One illustration is driving a car. When we first begin to drive, we consciously walk through all the behaviors—signaling, viewing the mirrors, gently merging into traffic, reading road signs, and so on. Over time, the routine tasks of driving require less conscious processing and our everyday commutes fall into regular patterns that do not actively engage our conscious processing. In the retail world, we all accept the basics of retailing that are routinely taught to new employees. We know the general layout of the stores, we expect to find certain items within defined categories, we expect sections to be blocked, and such. These shortcuts give us tools to navigate the complex store environment. Stores that fit our internal structures are "easy to shop" and will likely be revisited, all other things being equal. Those that do not fit the patterns are hard work and will fail. The Target store in Pasadena illustrates this phenomenon for us. The store is unusual in that it is one of the few multilevel stores in the chain. A few years ago, Target totally remodeled the store to make room for a food section. In doing so, they split the fashion merchandise on different floors so that, rather than having all the apparel in one location broken into children's, men's, and women's sections, they had women's apparel on the first floor and men's and children's clothing on the second. We logically understand the intent to link children's apparel with toys, sporting goods, and seasonal merchandise, thereby achieving the adjacencies we would expect in a more typical layout. However, the layout so violently conflicts with our internal sense of the way it should be, we never feel comfortable, and always experience a sense of having to work to figure out where things will be in the store. Consequently, we actively work to avoid going to the store, and our visitation is less than half what it used to be before the re-merchandising. We offer this not as a condemnation of the store layout that may be successful, but only as an example of the impact of internal patterns on shopping.

Consistency

Let's briefly visit one final sample from Roger Blackwell in an exercise that is typically run in large group settings.[8] On a sheet of paper, write the words in Figure 7.5 with coloured pens so that the color matches the word. On a separate piece of paper, repeat this list with the colors for the letters that do not match the word, so that red is written in blue ink, green is in red ink, and so on.

Red	Blue	Green	Orange
Green	Orange	Blue	Red
Red	Blue	Orange	Green
Orange	Green	Red	Blue
Blue	Red	Green	Orange

Figure 7.5 Consistency

Read the first list aloud.

Now repeat the process with the second set of words.

Typically, groups have no problem completing the first task. However, while groups generally start out correctly and in synch on the second chart, by the end of the first line execution starts to fail, and it totally disintegrates on the second line. What is happening is that when the words match the visuals, we process the information easily because it conforms to our expected norms. In the second example, the visuals do not match the verbal. We have to override the subconscious perception of color to complete the conscious processing of reading text. Our brains have to work hard to complete the task, and collectively we begin to fail early in the process. Compare this to your execution of marketing at retail material and the conformation to expected patterns for shoppers in the store.

Our brief examination of the application of research into how we process information illuminates five key points:

- Conscious processing is hard work and limited in scope. Consequently, we look for ways to increase our efficiency and ease our burdens.

- Information processing is deselective. We search for that which is relevant to our task at hand and exclude that which is not.

- What we "see" is different from what we observe, and our processing of information into meaningful segments is driven by a search for order that drives our interpretation and perception.

- We use patterns and structures to simplify complexity. Wherever possible, we move from a conscious consideration of every action to the employment of shortcuts to minimize our effort.

- Efficient processing breaks down when the conscious and subconscious do not synch. When our conscious processing does not match our subconscious expectation, our workload increases dramatically, we become fatigued, and performance deteriorates.

A recent personal experience for one of us highlights the application of many of these principles in the retail store. While preparing for a major holiday meal, I realized I did not have enough yeast for the planned amount of baking. I had already completed my major shopping trip to stock up for the meal. But, as typically happens, I needed to make a fill-in trip for the forgotten items and last-minute additions. My mental list was only five items, and my expectation was that I could complete my journey through the store in a few minutes. I grabbed a hand basket, picked up the first three items in produce, headed to the baking aisle, and stopped short. I could not find the yeast. I knew that the yeast was in this aisle because I shopped this store frequently. I knew that it was at eye level above the flour, and yet I could not find it; I could not find the empty hole to indicate it was out of stock, and I could not understand why I was having difficulty. I literally had to stop my anticipated pace of progress through the store and move consciously, item by item, across the shelf until I located the product. At last, after several painful seconds, I found my yeast and continued on.

Being immersed in the marketing at retail research, I naturally had to analyze what had occurred. For as long as I can remember, yeast had been packaged and merchandised in a horizontal package, as shown in Figure 7.6.

Figure 7.6 Expectation

Without realizing what I was doing, I was deselecting everything on the shelf that did not have this shape. When I discovered the item for which I was searching, it looked like Figure 7.7 on the shelf.

Everything was the same, except the square packets of yeast had been stacked to create a vertically oriented rectangle instead of the horizontal pattern I had in mind. I had created a heuristic for yeast that was based on its uniquely horizontal orientation on the shelf and excluded all the other potential visual clues such as color, logo, and so on. I recognized the space optimization associated with a more efficient use of the cube and then immediately wondered if the category had lost sales while shoppers built new visual associations with the product.

The search for yeast had become a task similar to searching for Waldo in a cartoon. The challenge for all retail marketing participants is to avoid creating their own Where's Waldo situations and, instead, define clear easy paths to find presentations, such as these in Figure 7.8.

Figure 7.7 Reality

Figure 7.8 Clearly Defined Sections

Logical

Although we all take shortcuts and respond to subconscious stimuli while in-store, the act of shopping is also a rational process. Roger Blackwell, formerly of The Ohio State University, published a number of studies that deal with the logical aspects of shopping. In general terms, as shoppers, we identify a problem, search for a solution to the problem, evaluate alternatives, and then make a choice. After consumption or use of the purchased product, we evaluate our satisfaction or dissatisfaction with our decision and incorporate that into our knowledge base for future evaluations (see Figure 7.9).[9]

Rational Consumer Behavior Model

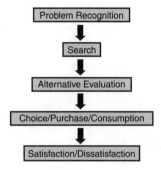

Figure 7.9 Logic

Of course, as we work through this process, we are confronted with a tremendous amount of marketing at retail that tries to persuade us to choose option A over option B and to pick up items C, D, and E along the way.

As Blackwell further dissects the logical aspects of a typical retail trip, we engage in groupings of behaviors. As we prepare to shop, we make lists and then decide which stores we will visit and the route we will take. We arrive at the store, and our experience is influenced by a host of influences including other shoppers, signage, traffic, parking ease, and more. As we continue into and through the store, our experience is affected by the people we meet and physical aspects of our journey. After our purchase decision is made, we continue to gather information and impressions formed by our experience in the process of checking out and exiting the shopping location. Together, these become part of our memory and play a role in our evaluation of alternatives when we are choosing a store in the future (see Figure 7.10).[10]

As we enter the store, we continue with a formal process of

Search ⟶ Identification ⟶ Evaluation ⟶ Selection

Consumer Behavior Model

Preparing to Shop	Arriving at Store	Entering Store	Shopping in Store	Checking Out	Transport and Storage
Make Lists	Environment	Entryway	Signage,	Time in line	Assistance with Loading
Choose Store	Parking Lot	Greeters	Lighting	Length of Line	
Plan Route	Safety	Security	Store Layout/	Payment	Ease of Leaving lot
Bundle Stops	Clientele	Cameras Familiarity	Flow	Methods	Disposal
Perceptions About Store	Signage	Ability to See Through Store	Aisle width	Monitoring	
Advertising	Lighting		Personnel Information	Price	
	Traffic		POP		
Past Experience			Price and Brand		

Figure 7.10 Consumer Behavior Model

We repeat this process until our mission is complete and our eventual basket likely contains a mix of planned and unplanned purchases, unless we are fulfilling a specific task. In total, we choose a store and decide on a navigation of that store, during which we make product category, brand, and quantity choices. These items then combine to create a total shopping basket for this trip, as depicted in Figure 7.11.

Figure 7.11 The Shopping Process

For most retail marketers, the parking lot would not seem to be near the top of any marketing consideration. However, the research shows that shoppers evaluate this criterion, often subconsciously, in terms of availability of parking, safety, and ease of exit, and that these considerations have an impact on sales. On the negative side, shoppers avoid a lot that is in disrepair as signaling that the store cannot be well-ordered within; they will also avoid an undersized parking lot during peak periods because cars line up in the road to jostle for parking.

At the other extreme is an example one of us experienced on a visit to the Pick and Pay Hypermarket in Durban, South Africa. I had heard from our hosts about how the parking lot experience enhanced the overall shopping trip and wondered how, outside of the typical access to convenient parking, this could be possible.

Upon arriving at the store's parking lot and much to my pleasant surprise, there was a uniformed greeter. He was not only welcoming me to the store, but he was also pointing me to a convenient parking space. He had the biggest, most sincere smile on his face, with one arm waving hello while the other pointed me to my spot. My immediate response was, if the store goes to this effort to make the shopper feel welcome outside of the store, I can only imagine the in-store experience. I was not disappointed and, for the first time, actually understood how an effort outside the location can affect perception of the inside of a store.

While making individual store selections, a number of other factors come into play, including

> **Weber's Law**—We evaluate things in relative versus absolute terms so that differences between options must be large enough to matter to us before they influence us to change our behavior.
>
> **Adaptation level theory**—We evaluate stimuli relative to the existing knowledge we have.
>
> **Perceived risk**—We compare the level of uncertainty about performance against the consequences of poor performance.
>
> **Personal accounting**—We incorporate our perception of losses versus gains on our internal scorecard.

Throughout our search for and acquisition of products, we move through an environment in which many more stimuli are presented than are seen; of those that are seen, fewer have meaning; of those that have meaning, even fewer result in a sale (see Figure 7.12).

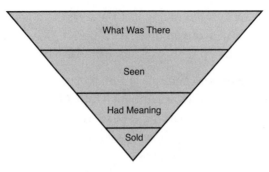

Figure 7.12 Engagement Model

As we process the store environment, we loathe dissonance and will go to great lengths to make things consistent in our minds. We search for experiences in tune with our expectations within the stores we select; we filter messages aggressively; we utilize the information we have; we weigh the risks and rewards; and, after taking action, justify our decisions and purchases while maintaining a personal scorecard.

With an understanding of logical shopper behavior as shoppers move through the store and fulfill their shopping goals, we can optimize our efforts:

	Characteristics	**Optimal Delivery**
Entering-the-Store Shopper	Assess store character	Clean
	Quick reads	Inviting
	First-decision point	Exciting
		Straightforward, simple messaging
In-Store Shopper	Orientation	Strong visual cues
	Decide to proceed or stop	Organize logically
	Move to shopping	Guide and enhance experience

Social

Expanding our area of focus, we now consider the role of social forces on the shopping process. As we have seen both in the previously cited studies and the field research in stores, the way shoppers make decisions is multilayered, and the relationship between consumers and marketers is complex. The communication between the two occurs at both conscious and subconscious levels with the weight of the subconscious far surpassing the conscious. Figure 7.13 depicts the relationship between shoppers and marketers:

Shopper Influences

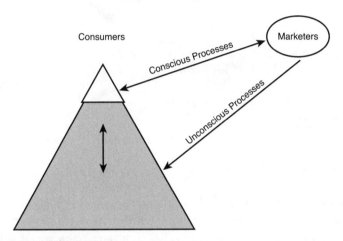

Figure 7.13 Shopper Influences

This process involves our attitudes, including the way we feel about a store or product, our intentions relative to the available shopping options, and our beliefs. Social forces play a significant role in shaping the attitudes that affect behavior. Although we have an ostensibly logical process for acquiring the products we want, it is influenced not only by the way we process information but also by social and group forces (see Figure 7.14).

As we move through the preceding elements, social and group forces work to mold our state of mind before shopping, while they also directly affect our actions at retail. For a reference point on the impact of social or reference groups, consider the persuasive power of the groups to which we belong in shaping our perception of what is hot or cool, or even necessary. Likewise, it is easy to observe the impact of a child on the items that end up in the shopping basket and the total basket size, or the power of a tightly knit clique of teenagers in driving actions in a Saturday trip to the mall.

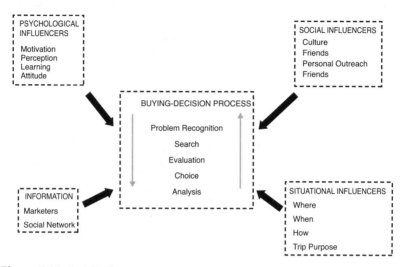

Figure 7.14 Social Influences

Social factors also play a role in our collection and processing of data. Beyond the information that retailers and manufacturers create and deliver, consumers and shoppers also seek data from social sources. These may be delivered on-line, in traditional media, or in person. The careful cultivation of early technology adopters for electronics, or rap stars and basketball players for the launch of the Cadillac Escalade, serve as witness to the social role in information gathering. Self-referential groups can remain relatively constant as they do for preteens or shift depending on the considered area; that is, geek friends for technology, music aficionados for music, and so on.

Finally, situational factors work to guide our decisions on why, where, when, and how we buy. These situational factors could be societal, like the chilling effect of a market recession on our willingness to make large purchases even though our individual purchasing capacity is not at risk. Or the factors could relate to a small group or individual. Our central point is that attitudes before we enter the store, our consumption of information, and our approach to shopping are influenced by a set of social influences that combine megatrends with self-composed reference groups.

As we assimilate these social influences, we tend to respond and pay attention to things that reinforce our world view and filter out the things that do not fit with that view. We remember things with personal significance, things that are consistent with our views of the world, and things that have either important consequences or associations.

We form perceptions of ourselves by observing our own behavior: "If I took this action, it must be rational." We evaluate choices with the available knowledge, but that information base extends beyond personal history and data points such as price references and brand imagery presented in stores to include social endorsements. Social forces shape our attitudes and choices of stores, brands, and products. In stores, these social forces can influence product selection, impulse buying, and brand switching. At the same time, situational factors affect our logical/economic shopping decisions and choices at all levels.

Consistency Versus Boredom

When we shop, we seek comfort in consistency and familiarity. However, a potential conflict arising in that sameness can breed boredom that can result in a loss of impulse sales as everything except the necessary is excluded from consideration. Shopping on autopilot provides a sense of comfort, but shoppers tend to not see anything outside of the mental list they are using to shop. Interrupting the autopilot creates dissonance.

This dissonance causes shoppers to "see" new things, opening them for purchase consideration at the same time that it causes stress by injecting thought into the shopping process. To optimize results, we need to balance the artful interruption of the shopping experience with the consistency shoppers expect.

Biologic Research

The biologic studies begin with the development of the brain over 280 million years of evolution. The team at ShopConsult, a German company that is a leader in the field, links the brain's development with its larger role in decision making. The brain stem, which is roughly 280 million years old, is our instinctual center and the locus of self-preservation behavior. The limbic system is our emotional center and dates to 165 million years ago. The center of "intelligence" or learning and memory is the cerebral cortex, which weighs in at a youthful 5 million years in age (see Figure 7.15).[11]

Biologic Brain Development

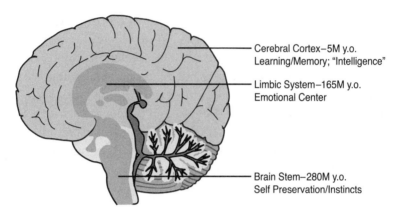

Cerebral Cortex–5M y.o.
Learning/Memory; "Intelligence"

Limbic System–165M y.o.
Emotional Center

Brain Stem–280M y.o.
Self Preservation/Instincts

Figure 7.15 Biologic Brain Development

By studying the neurological reactions to stimuli, the researchers can identify primary, secondary, and tertiary response levels. At the primary level we focus on safety and our base needs of food, sex, and shelter. This would describe the dominant operating system under times of deprivation or distress, where all other concerns shut down. A more standard level of operating in North America and the developed world has us moving through life at a social level in which we seek interaction and our limbic system is active. At peak performance levels, we seek discovery through physical or mental challenges that demand the processing of our cerebral cortex.

Our response to visual stimulation, likewise, triggers activity in different parts of the brain as we move from safety to social and discovery considerations. Negative or pain avoidance imagery triggers a reaction in the brain system, whereas social events activate the limbic system, and aspirational personal achievement stimulates the cerebral cortex.

Applying this learning to in-store marketing, the imagery used in display presentations triggers a variety of responses that create an emotional link to the brand and affect purchase. Consider the different options presented here: the depiction of a spoonful of medicine posed next to a professional physician-like bottle of elixir, as opposed to the display with no picture but just a category description, and then the presentation of a healthy baby. In the examples in Figure 7.16, the medicine is a means to an end—the way to achieve the smiling health of the last picture. The negative image of a bottle of medicine works against the brain stem, whereas the positive imagery of the happy infant activates the more developed regions of the brain.

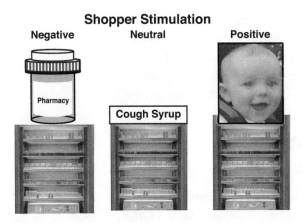

Figure 7.16 Shopper Stimulation

Summary

Moving beyond the field research that measured shopper's actions in-store with great precision, we reviewed some of the key academic research that applies to the shaping of shopper attitudes and behavior in stores. The research is broken into four categories:

- **Cognitive**—A review of the way we process information in general that applies directly to our collective and almost universal approach to dealing with the tremendous number of choices and messages we confront in a typical retail store.

- **Logical**—The task solution approach to the fulfillment of our product needs. This approach is related to classic economic theory that holds that all purchase decisions will be rationally based on our personal completion of a value equation for each choice (value = quality / cost).

- **Social**—A consideration of the interconnected relationships that shape our attitudes and behaviors in stores, affect our choice of credible information sources, and influence our decision on whether we should purchase and how we should purchase.

- **Biologic**—An evolutionary look at the underlying basis for our reaction to stimuli in the market that is influenced heavily by our need state while shopping.

Together, the academic research helps us understand the "why" behind the "what" that occurs in store. We know that a small fraction of the marketing material presented at retail is seen by the shopper. We now can understand how the advertising we present must work against the four areas of human psychology to be effective.

Endnotes

1. Roger Blackwell, *Retail Marketing*, Orlando, FL (2003).

2. Hugh Phillips http://www.instore-research.com/Images/Hugh%20PFB%20Presentation1.pdf, page 9.

3. Christopher Chabris and Ben Sherwood, *What it Takes to Survive* (New York: Crown Publishing, 2010) http://www.newsweek.com/2009/01/23/what-it-takes-to-survive.html.

4. Hugh Phillips http://www.instore-research.com/Images/Hugh%20PFB%20Presentation1.pdf, page 5.

5. Hugh Phillips, *The Power of Marketing at Retail*, (Alexandria, VA:, POPAI, 2008) 31.

6. Ibid., 32.

7. Hugh Phillips, *The Power of Marketing at Retail*, (Alexandria, VA, POPAI, 2008), pages 34–36.

8. Roger Blackwell, *Retail Marketing*, Orlando, FL (2003).

9. Ibid.

10. Ibid.

11. Christoph Haibock, *NeuroMarketing at Retail*, Dubai (2005).

8

Decision Drivers

Retail Factors and Purchase Decision Types

The retail store is a complex environment with thousands of messages presented in a confined space and in a compressed amount of time. As Figure 8.1 summarizes, the average shopper is presented with between 17 items per minute in relatively simple formats, such as a convenience store, and more than 300 items per minute in more complex environments such as grocery and chain drug stores. Confronted with an otherwise overwhelming amount of stimuli, shoppers necessarily employ a variety of coping mechanisms to effectively navigate their way through the store. Shoppers look for ways to simplify their trip and organize their experience. They seek out the marketing material that relates to their shopping mission and fits with the governing principles they believe are integral to this retailer (see Figure 8.1).[1]

Retail Success

	M@R Items	Min in Store	Items per Minute
Convenience	170	10	17
Drug	4759	15	317
Grocery	9378	30	313

Figure 8.1 Shopper Exposure

Financial Impact of Presentation Optimization

The financial impact of optimized performance is profound. Assume that 100 shoppers enter the store and 60 percent visit your aisle. Of these, half visit your section, and half of those visitors notice and interact with your product. Of these shoppers, one-third make a purchase and 40 percent purchase a related item.

Retail Success Steps

Choose your store	100
See/visit your aisle	60
See/visit your section	30
Notice/interact with your product	15
Purchase	5
Buy one more thing	2

If we improve our conversion by 20 percent at any single step along the process, we increase the total items purchased to 8.4. However, if we improve multiple areas simultaneously, the total rises to 18.4 items—more than double our base case (see Figure 8.2).

	Base Case	Ind 20% Inc	Ind 20% Inc	Ind 20% Inc	Ind 20% Inc	Ind 20% Inc	Cumulative 20% Improvement
Choose store	100	120					120.0
Visit aisle	60		72				86.4
Visit section	30			36			51.8
Interact with item	15				18		31.1
Purchase	5	6	6	6	6	6	12.4
Buy one more thing	2	2.4	2.4	2.4	2.4	2.4	6.0

Figure 8.2 Cumulative Improvement Impact

Shaping shopper behavior breaks complex activity into component parts and looks at techniques for motivating the desired behavior at each step of the compound retailing equation to improve results. For retail marketing, shaping is driven by increasing impact and engagement at each step.

Retail Success

Despite this message complexity, the path to retail success amounts to a combination of traffic and transactions. Quite simply, if you are a retailer, you have two ways to generate growth:

- Increase the number of transactions by:

- Generating more visits from existing customers

- Attracting new customers

- Converting more visitors who do not buy

Or

- Increase the transaction size with:

  - More items in the basket

  - A richer mix of higher priced items

This dynamic is shown in Figure 8.3.

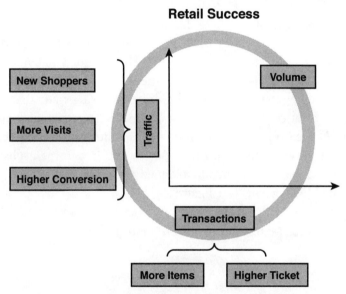

Figure 8.3 Retail Success Dynamic

The dynamic can be expressed as an equation in which volume is driven by the interplay between traffic and transactions:

$$\text{Traffic} \times \text{Transaction Value}$$

Traffic is defined as the number of shoppers times the number of visits per shopper divided by the shopper conversion rate. Transaction value is the number of items purchased times the average ticket value.

As the U.S. market continues to mature and major retailers exhaust the opportunities for physical expansion, same-store sales results will continue to be the key performance metric. Shopper intimacy provides shopper understanding. This understanding is the key to building greater value into our store offerings, and value drives growth:

$$\text{Shopper Value} = \frac{(\text{Emotional Payoff} + \text{Shopping Need Fulfillment})}{(\text{Cost} + \text{Effort})}$$

Apply this formula to the shopper behavior motivators we previously discussed. It is clear that retail practitioners must deliver more against shoppers' personal scorecards to capture a greater share of their spending.

Planned Versus Unplanned Purchases

The number of final purchase decisions made in-store offers a clear indication of the importance of retail marketing material. In its ground-breaking purchasing habits research, POPAI established that, in general, 70 percent of purchase decisions are made in-store. This finding was substantiated by the mass merchandising purchasing study that found that 29 percent of purchases in their channel were preplanned, and 71 percent of decisions were made in-store. This study further refined the groupings into specifically planned purchases (26 percent), substitute purchases (3 percent), generally planned purchases (18 percent), and unplanned (53 percent) (see Figure 8.4).[2]

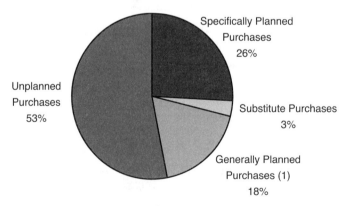

Figure 8.4 Purchase Decisions in Mass Merchandisers

While at Mattel, we found that the percentage of planned purchases varied widely by category, with a low of less than 20 percent for preschool toys in which the extended family makes a substantial portion of purchases and the recipient exerts no power in the decision-making process. By contrast, in outdoor play equipment planned purchases exceeded 80 percent because of the myriad of issues associated with transportation, placement of items in the yard, relatively high price point, and so on (see Figure 8.5).

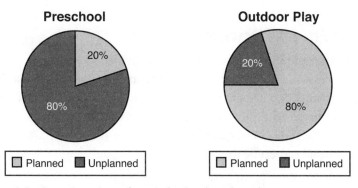

Figure 8.5 Planned Purchases for Preschool and Outdoor Play

Our view is that purchase decisions made in-store operate on a continuum with purely impulse buys at one end and items without substitute at the other (see Figure 8.6). As we move through different retail channels and categories of goods, the percentage of planned and unplanned purchases will vary. What does not change is the dynamic in which some items have no substitute, some are preferred but can be traded out, some are generally planned, some are decided in-store, and some are purely impulse.

Detroit, in addition to being the home of the automotive industry, is also the birthplace of Vernor's soda. In the area from Michigan through western Pennsylvania, drinking Vernor's is almost a religion, with a seemingly never-ending stream of serving variations, including its use as a soft drink, a mixer for alcoholic drinks, a base for ice cream floats, and a magical elixir to ease ailments. For us, and the denizens of this trading area, no substitute for Vernor's exists, and we move to other retail locations when it is delisted or out of stock. By contrast, for us, a cold bottle of water in a cooler at check-out represents an impulse purchase triggered by a recognition of our thirst in response to the cooler's presence at a location where we generally relax a bit at the conclusion of our shopping mission.

Planned Purchase Continuum

Figure 8.6 Purchase Decision Continuum

Retail Success Drivers

Store design and shopper navigation aids can play a key role in the shopping process. We can diagram the path to an eventual sale as a series of related actions that are the result of conscious and subconscious reactions that begin with the choice of store and reach its ultimate conclusion with the addition of one more item to the shopping basket. In the journey to sales success, the shopper must

- Choose your retail location.

- See and visit your aisle.

- See and visit your section.

- Notice and interact with your product.

- Then make a purchase decision.

To achieve real success in today's competitive marketplace, we need the shopper to also add one more item to the basket. To fulfill her shopping objectives, she evaluates the store exterior, aisle design, assortment, shelf organization, and selling aids presented throughout the in-store experience (see Figure 8.7).

To optimize the shopper experience and the return on the marketing investment in the store, marketers must align the success drivers with the retail decision steps, utilizing a REAP approach in which all participants' needs and desires are considered. Through this process we start with a consideration of the specific retailer as a unique environment and include the perspective of the personnel who play a critical role in executing and maintaining retail marketing programs. For retailers, these can include store operations, store managers, floor personnel, and others. For brands, internal constituencies might include the account management team, category management leads, or direct store delivery personnel.

Figure 8.7 Decision Steps and Drivers

Similarly, shoppers must be approached not as a uniform whole, but in as many meaningful segments as make sense for the marketing opportunity. The shopping process should be viewed through their unique eyes within the channel to develop insights, and these insights should routinely be incorporated into programs. The effectiveness of the programs must then be measured so that new insights can be developed resulting in the shopper intimacy we are all seeking (see Figure 8.8).

Retail Drivers—Store Exterior

Although store choice is impacted by a number of components outside of the store environment, the first physical presentation influencing store choice is the store exterior. In the days of the small town general store, it was enough to announce your presence. You were likely the only store in town, and most sales were assisted by the store clerk. It was assumed that the retailer would have all the items the market desired, and they received immediate feedback so that they knew whether gaps in the assortment existed. The market was largely captive, and fortunes rose and sank with that of the community served.

Retail Ecosystem Analytics Process

Constituencies (Retail/Brand)   Shopper Segmentation

Understanding/Insight

Process Integration

Intimacy

Figure 8.8 Retail Ecosystem Analytics Process (REAP)

Today's counterparts to the general store are the hypermarkets developed in Europe and in regional chains in the United States. For competitors such as Carrefour, Meijer, Walmart, and others, it is important to signal the ease of access to the tools you need to complete your shopping mission. Key factors can include availability of parking close to store entrances, the condition of the parking lot, shopping cart access, lighting, safety, and so on (see Figure 8.9). Compare the cluttered, cart-strewn Walmart entrance with the clean Best Buy store approach.

Walmart's store lot   **Best Buy's store exterior**

Figure 8.9 Store Exteriors

These factors and others help establish the store's character and signal the type of shopping experience to expect. Because we know that we all seek and reward consistency, we often see the remaking of store exteriors coincident with a store reset. For instance, when our local Vons was converted to a "Lifestyle" store inside, the exterior was updated and softened with the addition of more natural materials, such as field stone, to complement the more natural product presentation and color palette inside. The changed exterior forcefully signaled that things were different and reinforced the experience inside the store (see Figure 8.10).

Figure 8.10 Vons' Exterior Change

At the opposite end of the spectrum, an exterior can project a store's character as a niche player, such as a tack shop servicing horse lovers or an Apple store for technology aficionados. In each case, the exterior foreshadows what will be found inside, with a bucolic barn-like presentation for the country-minded riding set and an ultra-cool sleek and minimalist facade for Apple. Swapping these exteriors would not work because the barn would not accurately presage technology, nor would Apple's glass cube effectively signal riding equipment (see Figures 8.11 and 8.12).

Tack Shop Exterior   Interior Product Assortment

Figure 8.11 Tack Shop

Apple Store   **Interior Product and Genius Bar**

Figure 8.12 Apple Store

The store exterior can also signal an anticipated service level at both the low-end with the utilitarian entrance to a Tuesday Morning in stark contrast to Nordstrom's formally elegant entrance supported with valet parking (see Figure 8.13).

Figure 8.13 Store Exterior Signaling Service Level

The use of store exterior extends beyond chain stores to individual proprietors. A walk down the Boulevard Saint Germain in Paris during the holiday season is enough to make one want to stop and shop at every boutique. The tastefully decorated storefronts create a warm reception and invite shoppers to linger, relax, and enter the store.

Retail Drivers—Color Palette

As shoppers approach and enter the store, they are immersed in the store's color palette. Work completed by ShopConsult in Europe established the link between color palette and the mental states they trigger. Figure 8.14 breaks colors into four quadrants designated alpha, security, social, and explorer. At one extreme, matte colors signal security, whereas glossy presentations convey a sense of exploration. Alpha, leader responses are signaled by black, red and gold; security is conveyed with whites, green, and blues; our social impulses are triggered by oranges, pinks, and reds; and we connect with an explorer sensibility with light blues, silvers, and violets.[3]

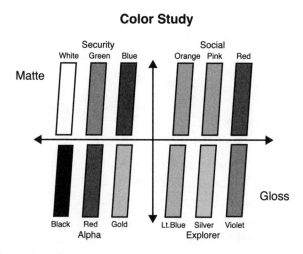

Figure 8.14 Color Influences

Color can also work as a marker for quality and price with bright colors in the lower quadrant and darker colors in the upper quadrant. With this understanding, it is not surprising that almost all premium cosmetic brands choose a high gloss for their retail presentations with colors from the alpha palette—Christian Dior and Chanel with glossy black, L'Oreal and Estee Lauder with high-gloss white and gold, and Elizabeth Arden with gloss red and white. The color palette simultaneously appeals to the targeted state of mind for their shoppers while establishing their quality level and pricing platform (see Figure 8.15).

Color Study

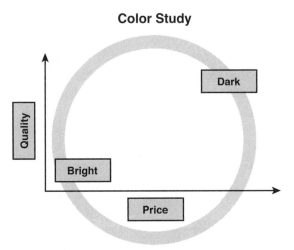

Figure 8.15 Color Study

When working with the chosen color palette, it is important to balance the weight of the execution. The pink in the Barbie packaging has a unique Pantone color assigned and is an integral part of the product's trade dress protected by law. In the research lab, we observed that girls were initially excited by their exposure to the packaging color.

However, if they were left in a room that was predominantly Barbie pink for a long time, they slipped into a type of sensory overload that quickly led to exhaustion. It was important for Mattel to balance the presence of pink in the aisle in both packaging and merchandising so that the requisite excitement was created without overwhelming the shopper's senses.

Retail Drivers—Store Layout/Navigation

Having entered the store, shoppers begin to orient themselves and begin their shopping mission. They make a choice as to how to move through the store and which sections of the store to visit. In general, in large retail formats, they confront store designs that either feature stacked aisles running from front to back or race track configurations. The stacked aisle arrangement depicted in Figure 8.16 maximizes the amount of product that can be presented in the available floor space, whereas the race track design maximizes the distance traveled by shoppers.

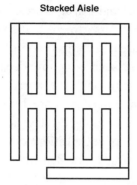
Stacked Aisle

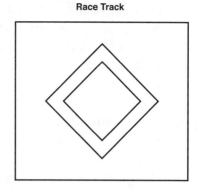
Race Track

Figure 8.16 Store Layouts

Returning to the example of the general store, in a shopping environment in which a clerk assisted in product selection and the choices were relatively narrow, access to product was the key success determinant and maximizing the items offered optimized the store's success. Stores were characterized by a single entrance with the cash drawer at the front, and merchandise was densely packed with a uniform aisle width around the perimeter and within, as shown in Figure 8.17.

General Store Layout

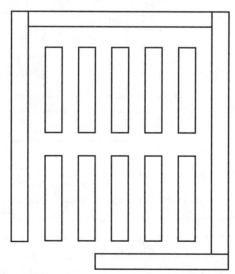

Figure 8.17 General Store Layout

This remains the dominant layout for most chain drug stores. This channel predominantly presents a merchandise assortment that spans a wide variety of food and general merchandise in a compact footprint. They generally feature an anchor in one corner, such as a photo department. Recognizing the value of driving traffic through the store, they almost universally position the pharmacy in the rear of the store. In large stores, impulse items may be presented in free-standing displays across the front of the store; in smaller formats, the shopper transitions directly from the core merchandise area to the cash wraps. The density of the product offering in the available space dictates a layout in which SKU presentation is maximized, and these stores generally make extensive use of high gondolas (see Figure 8.18).

Chain Drug Layout

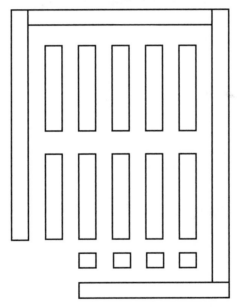

Figure 8.18 Chain Drug Store Layout

Traditionally, grocery stores also deal with high SKU counts in confined areas, offering roughly 45,000 SKUs in a mean store size of 47,500 square feet. The old-line traditional grocery store shown in Figure 8.19 was marked by a densely merchandised core of packaged items surrounded by a perimeter of dairy, meat, and fresh fruit and vegetables. Understanding the value of directing traffic flow throughout the store, grocers arranged their products so you had to travel to each corner of the store to fulfill a typical shopping trip that might include bread, butter, milk, fruits, vegetables, and meats. The resultant layout is similar to a general store with the addition of cases for meat in the rear of the store and fresh produce on one side. In their quest for efficiency, shoppers learned to navigate these stores by pushing their cart around the exterior and darting into selected core aisles, often without their shopping baskets.

Traditional Grocery Layout

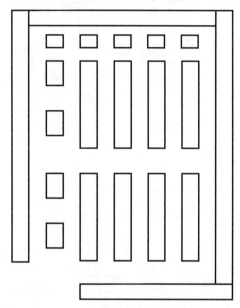

Figure 8.19 Traditional Grocery Store Layout

Although retailers have long realized the value of motivating shoppers to move throughout the store, thereby increasing their exposure to product choices and increasing the likelihood of an incremental item in the basket, they now also appreciate the role design can play in altering shoppers' moods. Grocery market leaders now understand that store productivity is further enhanced by slowing shoppers down both mentally and physically, so they are in a more relaxed state when confronting product choices and marketing messages. As a supplement to their four-corner product placement strategy, these operators now create places to linger that fully engage the senses. In these stores, the perimeter is not an area to be traversed but a place to luxuriate in the sensuousness of food. These grocers present floral shops, bakeries, tea counters, artisanal cheese sections, olive bars, fresh nut roasters, and on and on (see

Figure 8.20). In each case, our senses are appropriately engaged—we are shopping for food and the store becomes a celebration of food. Subconsciously, we slow a little, and the physical space creates an incentive to linger and explore versus traversing through the location on the way to the next item in our literal or mental shopping list.

Modern Grocery Store Layout

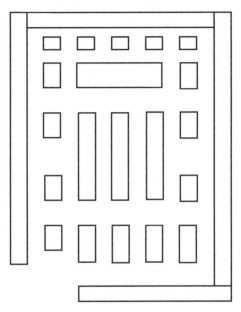

Figure 8.20 Contemporary Supermarket Layout

As we move to general merchandisers, we see a dramatic shift away from the stacked aisles that typified general stores. Although the goal remains to expose shoppers to the maximum number of product choices, the tactical execution shifts. Instead of traveling around a perimeter of densely packed aisles, shoppers are now directed to travel along a "race track" around the store, as shown in Figure 8.21. The advantages of this approach include the orderliness of the path so that we intuitively accept the direction; the efficiency of the path in that we do not have to move through the entire store perimeter; and the flexibility of the navigation enabling multiple points of entry and departure. In some large retail formats, a center aisle may bisect the race track but, in general, it is difficult to crisscross through the store by traveling directly from one corner to the other and, even where it is possible, the path is not clear. In some retailers, the race track is kept clean of all interruptions so that shoppers can move unimpeded through their tasks, and attention is focused on the individual product sections. In other retailers, the "power aisle" is interrupted repeatedly with large product presentations supported with marketing at retail designed to move significant amounts of product.

Typical Race Track Examples

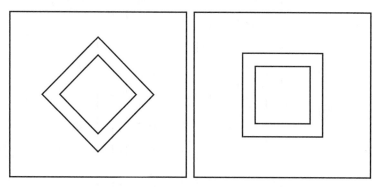

Figure 8.21 Race Track Layouts

Regardless of the store layout chosen, the studies conducted by Paco Underhill and his associates at Envirosell have clearly shown us that we all follow a predictable pattern in addressing a new physical environment.[4] Typically, we move through the first phase of the physical space and, after we have sufficiently entered the environment, we slow down and begin our mission. The process works in stores where we shop, theme parks where we go to escape, and trade shows where we look for ideas and to make business connections.

In retail stores, shopper orientation to the physical environment has the potential to create dead zones. Toys R Us offers a relevant case study of the issue and a successful solution to transforming a dead zone. Toys R Us was built on the grocery store/general store stacked aisle layout model. With a single entrance, the store directed shoppers to a cart pick-up location and then through an area in which party supplies were merchandised on the lower wall, and seasonal goods, promotions, and special values were presented in two display lanes down the center (see Figure 8.22). The thought was that shoppers would follow an "S" shaped pattern as they moved through the foyer filling their carts with the presented items on the way to their core mission (see arrows). The merchants were surprised when store observation revealed that shoppers picked up their carts and raced through one of the aisles hardly breaking their pace until they reached the store core.

Old Toys R Us Layout

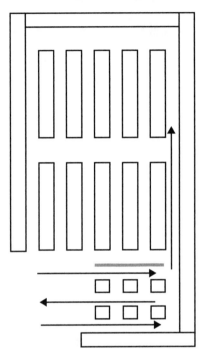

Figure 8.22 Old Toys R Us Layout

To make productive use of the selling space, Toys R Us accepted that shoppers would move through a corridor on their way to the store core. They moved the upper wall down to create a single aisle that was lined with the party supplies that were a destination product—if you had a party, you would stop or revisit the area to select the products you needed. They transformed the newly created space into two "feature area locations" (see Figure 8.23). These were stocked with topical products supporting the latest movie or product release or a key seasonal event such as Back to School. The product displays were supplemented with an aggressive retail marketing campaign so that shoppers were more likely to notice the goods. The result was that, as shoppers entered the core, they saw the displays, visited the areas, and purchased the products. What had been largely unproductive space became some of the most productive real estate in the store as the marketing presentation interrupted shopper's thought pattern and caused them to mentally slow down.

New Toys R Us Layout

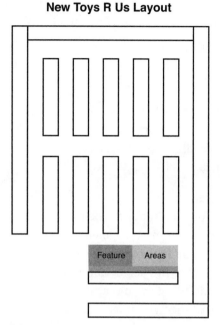

Figure 8.23 New Toys R Us Layout

Retail Drivers—Assortment

The product presented within the store layout plays a vital role in supporting the store brand. The assortment can be broad or narrow across the categories presented, or it can be deep or shallow in the number of item choices within each category. Either way, the assortment must present a strong value to the shopper in meeting her needs for her chosen shopping occasion, and it must be consistent to support repeated visits.

Supercenters and pharmacies pursue different paths in presenting broad categories of goods—supercenters present a relatively deep selection, whereas drug stores have relatively narrow item options for noncore segments such as automotive or toys. The promise from each is convenience, but a supercenter is positioned as a destination for major shopping trips, whereas drug stores provide a fill-in function.

Merchandise specialists offer deep assortments in a narrow grouping of related categories. These can take multiple forms, such as the following:

- Category specialists such as Bed Bath & Beyond, Staples, or The Home Depot, each focusing on a functional category.

- Lifestyle retailers such as Zumiez for skateboarding, surfing, and snowboarding; Hot Topic for teenage goths, Twilight, and music fans; or Lush for hand-crafted bath items.

- Branded retailers whether narrowly centered on a market segment, such as Lush; or market segment, such as Abercrombie & Fitch; or broadly directed against a category, such as health and performance for Nike.

The differential strategies are roughly depicted in Figure 8.24. Extreme operators such as Aldi and warehouse clubs tighten their product offerings to a single option in many segments; that is, one size of Kellogg's Corn Flakes or a single brand choice for plastic bags. They offset the narrowed selection with the perception of ultra value so that shoppers make a mental trade-off of savings against the limited selection. As we noted in our view of the market dynamics, the middle is an extremely difficult position to hold, and a premium is attached to clearly owning an assortment space.

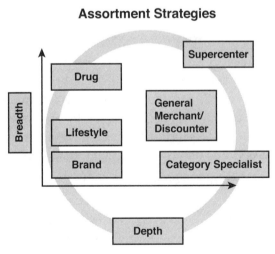

Figure 8.24 Assortment Strategies

Retail Drivers—Adjacencies

Product assortment is the fundamental building block that often defines and always supports the store brand positioning to attract and retain a base of both dedicated and occasional shoppers. The organization of that assortment into logical adjacencies can influence the acceptance of the desired brand positioning by

- Intuitively meeting shopper's needs and expectations
- Enhancing performance by:
  - Raising the average shopping basket value
  - Efficiently supporting the shopping process

The operative organizing principle for virtually all retailers holds that items should be grouped into logical categories, with categories broken into meaningful sections and items rationally arranged within each category. When executed properly, we leverage the shopper's need-state in the product section so that she increases her shopping basket size by making an incremental purchase related to the first selection. An example would be the location of mayonnaise, ketchup, mustard, and pickles in adjacent areas so that the purchase of one might trigger the purchase of other items that could be related to sandwich making. Sears defined the hierarchy as

Group ⟶ Department ⟶ Line ⟶ Sub-Line ⟶ Item

Although this process seems tremendously simple, it is often complicated by either an inability to clearly identify the logical home for an item or a lack of organizational focus on the shopper.

Examples of the first instance include a consideration of placing mixers such as ginger ale in the liquor aisle or the carbonated beverage aisle; the placement of isotonics with carbonated beverages or water; the location of popcorn in the salty snack or cracker areas. Adjacency decisions in each case can have a dramatic impact on sales. As we witnessed in the MARI studies, shoppers do not see products presented in areas where they do not expect to find them. By contrast, location in the proper section can significantly boost sales.

The second failure occurs when the buying structure does not align with the shopper's expectation of where to find products. In the situation depicted in the Figure 8.25, the shopper focus is lost as buying assignments are made based on logical supplier relationships or the desired balancing of seasonal workloads. In these instances space is given to a vice president, who breaks it between the divisional merchandise managers, who divide it among their senior buyers, who then allocate to their buyers. It is easy to lose sight of the shopper experience as each level works with internal focal points on supplier and workload management.

Organization – Buying Structure

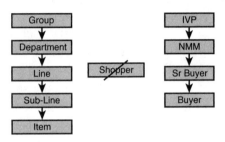

Figure 8.25 Organizational Buying Structure

A real-world example presented itself in the case of the toy department at a major discounter. In working a category management analysis, we analyzed the departmental layout from the shopper perspective. Shoppers are in the market for preschool toys, defined by age, girl's or boy's toys delineated by gender, or family fun toys that were appropriate for both sexes and a wide range of ages. For example, if you shop for a girl, it is obviously easiest to move through all the options for girls and family fun, but you would have no interest in boys or preschool products. Defining each category by color, we discovered an extraordinarily inefficient departmental design in which colors were mixed, and shoppers needed to move throughout the entire department to consider all the options of interest to them (see Figure 8.26).

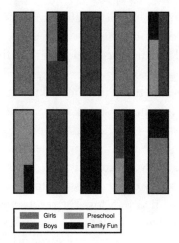

Figure 8.26 Old Adjacencies

Without increasing the space for the department or any category or section, we suggested a more shopper-centric layout in which the boy's products were adjacent to one another; all the girl's products were in the same area; and the family fun section bridged the two areas. Shoppers only in the market for single-sex products could now easily move from their targeted section to the gender neutral area, and those who needed to shop the entire department could more easily consider their options. The result was increased sales productivity from an identical assortment. Significantly, the retailer also reaped major cost savings by reducing the number of sections that needed to move for each reset (see Figure 8.27).

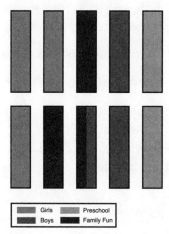

Figure 8.27 New Adjacencies

A consideration of how to handle a major license at the retail level offers a second powerful lesson on the power of proper adjacencies. While at Sears, we secured a major license for Disney that had tremendous application to the toy department. The buying group developed scores of exclusive products, and the marketing group decided we should make a theatrical presentation in the stores and catalogs by grouping all the Disney-themed products together in a single section. The move was protested by a seasoned buyer who predicted that an out-of-category presentation of product would negatively affect sales. Emboldened by the success of the recently opened Disney stores, we ignored the warning and created the themed sections. The results were disastrous. As the veteran buyer had predicted, items with a long track record of consistent sales fell 20 percent, and the results were consistent in both retail and catalog. The following year, when we put the items back where the shopper expected to find them, sales returned to normal levels. Clearly, shoppers were in the market for a category of goods and made their selection from the proffered items; they were not in the market for a licensed toy in which they would make a choice between different expressions of that license.

Retail Drivers—Shelf Organization

With our adjacencies decided, we turn our attention to the physical arrangement of the product on shelf (planogram). As we consider planogram development, it is helpful to briefly revisit the academic research. Two key learnings from the research provide powerful insights that can be leveraged to optimize item presentation on the shelf:

- Our continual quest for establishing order in our physical world

- Our approach to shopping as a deselection process

Our brains are magnificently efficient at processing information and creating meaning from the stimuli with which we are presented. We subconsciously process clues and, if elements are missing, we "intuitively" fill in the blanks. This mental process occurs both verbally and visually.

Consider the following sentence:

"I wnt to th stre to by mlk and btter but cme bck wth beer."

Even though the statement is missing eight critical vowels, few people have any issue with correctly interpreting the characters as the following sentence:

"I went to the store to buy milk and butter but came back with beer."

The process happens extraordinarily quickly and without the application of conscious effort.

We apply the same type of processing to visual cues so that we "see" the four dots in Figure 8.28 as a square:[5]

Figure 8.28 Physical Arrangement Example

Similarly, just as most people connect the dots to form a square, we interpret Figure 8.29 as a circle by editing out the interruption.

Figure 8.29 Physical Arrangement Example

Our search for order and organization extends to planograms in-store. In the real-world example from Hugh Phillips, Ph.D., in Figure 8.30, the liquor department was organized with a gin section on the top two shelves, a rum section on the bottom two shelves, and a large whiskey assortment that extended vertically down all five shelves to the right of the other two sections and interrupted the gin and rum presentation on the middle shelf.[6]

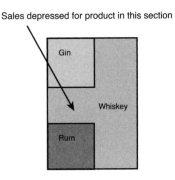

Sales depressed for product in this section

Figure 8.30 Physical Arrangement Case Study

No matter which product was placed between the gin and the rum, sales were depressed in what became a dead zone. With a choice between right and left sections for whiskey, the dominant side wins, and we simply do not "see" the area that does not fit with the order we establish (see Figure 8.31).

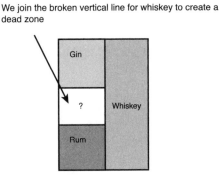

We join the broken vertical line for whiskey to create a dead zone

Figure 8.31 Physical Arrangement Case Study

In the western world, we process information as we read, from left to right and top to bottom. We seek cues from our physical environment to establish order and subconsciously apply patterns to the cues presented to create our personal order. We edit out what doesn't fit and do not see anything that conflicts with the order we impose on the retail presentation with which we are presented.

The second key piece of research deals with our deselective approach to shopping. In our quest for efficiency, we use patterns to subconsciously process information so that we can, in effect, parallel process data and multitask. In the store environment, we accomplish this by scanning the environment to locate broad clues for our desired product, applying our internalized patterns, so that we can then narrow our search on a particular area and then find the sought item.

Dr. Hugh Phillips describes the phenomenon as a macroscanning process, as shown in Figure 8.32. In the shopping environment, we move from subconscious to conscious processing as we begin browsing the store, and move through a deselection process that guides us to a section, an aisle, a shelf, and finally an item. Our processing moves from the general to the detailed as we increasingly sharpen our focus. When the first task is complete, we repeat as much of the process as necessary.[7]

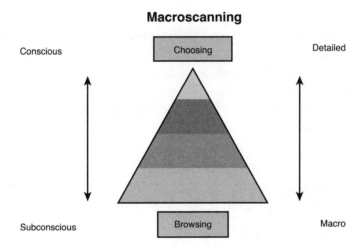

Macroscanning

Conscious · Choosing · Detailed

Subconscious · Browsing · Macro

Figure 8.32 Macroscanning

Several labs have consistently tracked the macroscanning process across multiple media. As shoppers, our utilization of this search function is also reinforced by eye-tracking studies performed in both North America and Europe. We scan a wide area so that we process key elements across multiple categories that might provide the cues that trigger our stored patterns. As we locate key elements, we move to a more detailed consideration in a "narrow" scan mode. The store data in our cognitive research section shows that attempting to deal with an entire store item by item would be overwhelming and consume more time and effort than practicable, so we take shortcuts. The easier we make the process, the more relaxed and less fatigued the shoppers will be. Relaxation and reduced fatigue translate directly into more sales.

As we move through our macroscanning process, we search for signposts. These verbal and visual cues help us find our way to the things we want to consider in detail. We seek efficiency in our processing and look for the easiest path to complete our mission. In some cases, a unique packaging approach, such as the generalized shape of a ketchup bottle, provides the trigger for identifying the sought-after product grouping. For many categories or subcategories, the dominant brand often defines the category, providing both emotional and visual cues. In these cases, well-known brands and symbols provide effective signposts-so that a prominent display of these brands can increase total category sales by attracting increased attention. Conversely, a weaker presentation can depress sales.

In the United Kingdom, ShopConsult tracked the impact of shelf location on total category sales. The dominant brand of beans is highlighted in the Figure 8.33. When the brand was moved from waist to floor level, total category sales dropped 16 percent. With a weaker visual presentation of the dominant brand, fewer shoppers "saw" the section, and this decrease drove total sales down.[8]

Organization–Dominant Brand

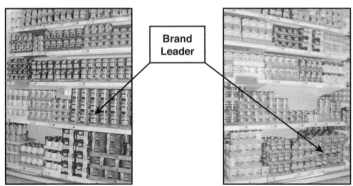

Brand Leader

Figure 8.33 Dominant Brand on Lowest Shelf

Understanding how shoppers use leading brands as signposts, we gain new insight into the MARI findings related to the height of the observed retail marketing material. Traditionally, retailers placed brands in the least desirable shelf location to maximize the visibility for high-margin private label items. The research suggests retailers are better served by moving key brands to more visible shelf locations and positioning alternative offerings side by side. In this manner shoppers can easily find the category (enhancing total sales), and the alternative product is more likely to be seen as attention starts to drift. Additionally, the retailer eases the shopper into a possible consideration of a value calculation and, by making shopping easier, reduces fatigue, increasing the likelihood that she buys an additional item (see Figure 8.34).

Lead brand on lower shelf   **Private label side by side with lead brand**

Figure 8.34 Dominant Brand Side by Side

Multiple eye-tracking studies conducted both in stores and under lab conditions show the importance of focusing attention. Whether studying our interaction with media at home or in retail stores, researchers consistently found that we initially direct our attention to the intended item but, if something else draws interest, our attention shifts. In Figure 8.35, the shopper located the Tylenol she sought on the shelf. Eye-tracking studies, as shown in Figure 8.35, reveal that when she found her desired product, she did not remain fixated on it but continued to move about the desired object in all directions.[9]

As Dr. Hugh Phillips observed in Figure 8.36, after locating the desired Tylenol, the shopper briefly considered analgesic options and then settled on the large dump display for Tylenol before finalizing her purchase. We screen out everything unrelated to our mission until we locate the item we seek and then our attention starts to drift. The key to optimizing sales is to assist in the efficient search for each subline or subcategory and then work to leverage the opening in our attention span to motivate an incremental purchase.

Figure 8.35 Shopper Focus

Figure 8.36 Shopper Focus-Natural Drift

It is critical that we maintain clean lines and logical breaks in our product presentation. We know that shoppers search for recognizable patterns and impose an order on the shelf presentation if one does not logically exist. We can assist this process and hold the attention in the section by bookending a display with formal breaks. These can take the form of a special unit within the gondola run or a formal signage system that provides verbal and visual cues for shoppers. Similarly, we can create a section within a section, such as the dip treatment in Figure 8.37, which both divides two subcategories of salty snacks (kettle chips and healthy snacks) while drawing focused attention to an assortment of complementary dips.

Bookending   **Dip Divider**

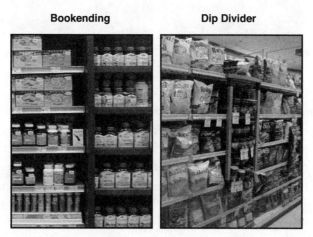

Figure 8.37 Vertical Segmentation

Another case study from Dr. Phillips shows the power of a planogram that properly focuses attention. In this case, nothing was changed between the two examples in Figure 8.38 except the physical alignment of the product. The items stayed the same, as did the facings and the marketing at retail support. Yet, by altering the presentation so that it was more visually pleasing and more "intuitive" to shop, sales increased 37 percent.[10]

A case study from the bicycle accessories category at a major discounter provides another example of the significance of proper section organization. The placement of items on the shelf had been driven by the sales team located in the retailer's city and led by the account executive.

Figure 8.38 Shelf Organization

This manufacturer dominated the section, and the retailer was happy to let them, as the category expert, drive the planogram. Unfortunately, the category team was fixated on maximizing the SKUs listed by cramming everything that could fit into the designated 16-foot section. The category team had a shelf section set up in their offices, and they would work for hours arranging and rearranging the product so that they could squeeze one more item on the peg board. The result was a total intermingling of unrelated products in a presentation with maximum product density and a complete lack of shopper focus.

Working with the headquarters marketing team, we addressed the product line in terms of a macro-sort. We defined three product groupings: safety, repair, and accessories. We arranged the products within each of these groupings and created a clean vertical break for each section. We arranged the products so that repair anchored one end of the display, accessories secured the opposite end, and safety was positioned in between (see Figure 8.39). The accessories and repair products were small and created a dense presentation; the safety products were large. By balancing the small products on either end with the large in between, we made the section feel less daunting. The accessories were "want" items approached casually, whereas the repair products were a "need" items. The repair items were also somewhat technical—the shopper had a problem to be solved and was on a hunt for a solution and would, therefore, be task focused. The helmets bridged shopping occasions as either a potential replacement purchase, or a related item purchase accompanying the acquisition of a new bike. By positioning the accessories adjacent to the helmets, we hoped to catch shoppers in a more relaxed browsing state while they were completing their total purchase.

The rationale to all the involved parties was that the real key was not how much went on the shelves, but how much moved off them. SKUs and facings were reduced to deliver a planogram that was cleaner and more focused. The program was tested against control stores and resulted in a doubling of sales.

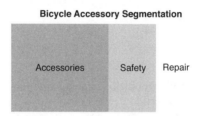

Figure 8.39 Section Organization Case Study

Leveraging Related Items

An important part of the planogram consideration for bicycle accessories was leveraging the state of mind for a segment of the purchasers of safety products to create incremental sales. We know from the research that shoppers want meaningful retail conversations in a context that works for them as individuals. We wanted to structure our merchandise conversation with shoppers who were completing their purchase of a new bicycle so that it was easier for them to add a few more items to accessorize their new purchase while they were in a state of mind open to considering the additional items. The results clearly reinforced our contention that shoppers will reward marketers who assist them in making connections that make it easier to complete their shopping task.

Shopper Segmentation

Shoppers can be segmented in many ways:

- Age

- Sex

- Ethnicity

- Income

- Household size

- Children in home

- Type of trip

- Need state

- Frequency of store visit

- Dollar spend

The key is to understand the individual in our particular retail context so that we can better anticipate and serve her needs. Depending on audience characteristic at a particular time, a product may be classified as a need (planned list item) or want item (impulse product). As the bicycle accessory program shows, properly leveraging need products for greater impulse sales can dramatically improve results.

A need product is a driver for a shopping occasion—I need to go to the store because.... Often these products are decidedly unglamorous. Examples can include items that are almost always a need-based product, such as printer cartridges, wiper blades, or items in which the classification may vary between need and want depending on the audience or occasion, such as fresh coffee you "need" in the morning, but occasionally use as a self-reward in the afternoon. Need items drive lists which, in turn, motivate shopping trips. As such, they are the creators of the traffic that defines opportunity at retail.

Want products are the items that are not necessary to our primary mission. Often they are added on during the shopping trip. They are sometimes indulgences or provide immediate, psychic gratification, such as a high-definition television in the printer cartridge outlet, wheel covers or car accessories at the wiper blade store, or pastries with the fresh coffee.

Want items leverage the opportunity provided by need traffic to build the shopping basket.

Campaigns to build the shopping basket are enhanced by reaching the shopper when she has moved from the macroscanning/browsing mode to a consideration of items for purchase. When she enters this mode and begins to scan across the item presentation, she is more easily reached, and she is reached most easily when the secondary item relates to the primary purchase. At times the connection is obvious, as with complementary products such as, hot dogs/buns or wine and meat. At other times the connection may have more to do with a need state for shoppers in-store. Thus, appetizer or dinner roll suggestions work well with the presentation of a holiday main course such as ham or turkey as shoppers look to round out their meal. Similarly, a co-location of diapers and beer works in convenience stores that are shopped mostly by men. The young father goes in to buy diapers and rewards himself with a six-pack of beer, or he goes to buy beer and attempts to endear himself to his spouse with the additional acquisition of diapers. Whether they are motivated by the specifics of the items, a shopping occasion, or the demographics of a targeted shopper group, the driver for increasing sales is reaching the shopper when she is open to suggestion. The success of our efforts is determined by their relevance, visibility, and execution as they relate to the shoppers in your store.

Shelf Alignment

One final planogramming consideration is shelf height alignment. The more shoppers see, the more they will purchase, and a critical part of getting them to see more is to attract them from the perimeter or the race track into additional sections. From the previous examples, we have seen that shoppers react to an orderly presentation of product. Maintaining disciplined shelf heights creates a cleaner line that is easier for the shopper to process and invites more browsing down aisles.

Consider the three examples in Figure 8.40. The towels in the first picture are presented with a consistent shelf configuration and separated vertically by color, whereas the health and beauty section from a supermarket maintains shelf discipline even with items of vastly different sizes. By contrast, the learning aids in the toy department have different shelf heights every eight feet. The learning aids require more mental processing to shop.

Some retailers, such as Target, go to extraordinary lengths to maintain a single shelf height for an entire gondola run, even asking manufacturers to change packaging sizes. Others focus on the existing product attributes and position the shelves to maximize the items that can be presented.

Sections with height discipline

Learning aids with variable heights

Figure 8.40 Shelf Alignment Examples

Purchase Drivers—Overview

Purchase drivers are the specific tools we can employ to attract more shoppers and motivate them to engage with our products and then purchase them. The key to improved effectiveness lies in optimizing each step of the shopping process. We rely on five techniques to drive purchases. Retail marketing effectiveness comes from properly employing one or more of these elements in a time and manner that are relevant to the shopper:

- Visibility

- Access

- Ease of purchase

- Communication/education

- Involvement

As we work with each of these drivers, we try to inject emotional power into our campaigns and transform suboptimal legacy presentations into high-performing marketing and product offerings.

Visibility

Visibility relates to our ability to see items and their marketing support, either on-shelf or in a feature location. The research shows us that shopper engagement increases in relation to the relevance of the message, and that relevance includes both location and the information communicated so that visibility is a function of what, where, and how we receive communication.

After entering the store, shoppers orient themselves and map their visit. In smart retailers, marketing elements support this process. Marketing material designed to be read from 300 feet away attracts shoppers to the area; from a distance of 30 feet marketing material draw shoppers to the particular section; and marketing messages designed to be read from 3 feet away help close the sale.

Frito-Lay drove category results by supporting this process. They created overhead signage to mark the aisle location and ensure that shoppers could find their products' location in store. They then sorted their items into four shopper-focused groupings: lunch, meal preparation, healthy snacking, and traditional snacks (see Figure 8.41). They created logical groupings by usage occasion to make it easier for shoppers; they arranged the items to make it easy for the shopper fulfilling a primary purchase need to also consider a secondary purchase, such as meal preparation next to snacks, or meal preparation adjacent to healthy snacks as a reward, and so on. The total presentation package was supported with way-finding signage to locate the aisle, graphics overhead to trigger an emotional response, and section markers to quickly identify the location of the category for which shoppers were searching. When the shopper was in the right section, packaging and shelf signage closed the sale.

Snack Aisle Segmentation

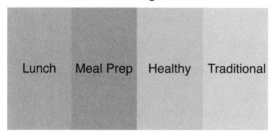

Figure 8.41 Snack Aisle Segmentation

Out of the main aisle, increased visibility can be accomplished by linking with a related product. You can tie your product to an event with which your product shares a connection or other related products. The key is to position displays and marketing material in locations where shoppers are open to the products and messages proffered. Figure 8.42 shows related items such as an in-line presentation of chips and salsa, a Guinness tie-in with St. Patrick's Day, and a bulk display that highlights the distinctive Miller bottle shape along with visuals that reinforce the enjoyment associated with consuming the beverage. Visibility improved results by increasing the number of shoppers who saw both the first item and related items.

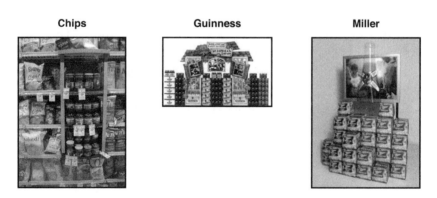

Figure 8.42 Cross-Merchandising

Other examples of properly using visibility as a driver include a gigantic billboard created with Thanksgiving serving platters at the entrance to a Bed, Bath, and Beyond, and a virtual coconut tree created with coconut water in Whole Foods (see Figure 8.43).

Thanksgiving Platters

Coconut Tree

Figure 8.43 Product as Visual Billboard

Access

Greater access increases sales by simplifying the purchase process by making the product more widely available to shoppers in locations they expect to find it. In the convenience store study, researchers found that marketing for single-serve salty snacks was particularly effective at the food service counter. The shopper was open to the message offered as he decided on his meal purchase, and access to the product in this area naturally complemented the shopper's orientation in this place, at this time. Similar phenomena are seen in large stores with cold beverage coolers at the front of the store, single-serve candy and gum packages at check-outs, or candy and popcorn offered in Blockbuster locations. In each case, access to product was increased to provide a complement to the experience, be it a meal, movie, or refreshment and reward at the end of a shopping journey.

Ease of Purchase

By making it easier to consummate a purchase, we increase sales. This can take the form of providing additional self-service options to make a quick purchase, grouping items so that a "complete purchase" can be made more efficiently, or removing impediments to purchase. In full-service retail, cosmetics had traditionally been sold through a counter with assistance provided by a sales clerk. Over the last ten years, a major trend was the introduction of open-sell product presentations, where shoppers could opt to make their selections by themselves and pay for the product (see Figure 8.44). By not requiring shoppers to work with a sales associate, sales were increased as shoppers gained direct product access. In a similar vein, supermarkets have created a profitable business segment in complete meal solution centers. Counter to the usual impulse to motivate shoppers to travel across the entire store, these presentations make it easy to put together a complete meal by visiting only one section of the store. These can be expressed in many forms, from all-in-one pasta centers to expanded hot food sections (see Figure 8.45). The converse is seen when theft deterrents are introduced at retail. Whether these are locked cases, pull tags, or interactive mechanisms that prevent shoplifters from emptying entire shelves of high-value products in one motion, the introduction of another step in the sales process, although it reduces shrinkage, uniformly decreases sales (see Figure 8.46).

Figure 8.44 Assisted Versus Open Sell

All-in-One Pasta Center

Home Meal Center

Figure 8.45 Meal Centers

Figure 8.46 Theft Deterrents

Education

Education builds revenue by imparting essential information on considered purchases to interested shoppers. The chain drug study highlighted the positive impact of educational information on vitamin sales in that channel. Products that are complex or offer a variety of options benefit from providing succinct sales support information. The delivery mechanism may be simple signage, such as the definition of a good/better/best line structure, instructions on how to properly fit your child to the proper bicycle, or technical data to support your decision to purchase top-of-the-line audio equipment (see Figure 8.47). Alternately, the execution can be more complex, as in the interactive video program that supported the construction of a personalized DirecTV package created through a series of prompts delivered via a touch-screen kiosk (see Figure 8.48). The key is that it is appropriate to the category, contains the proper level of detail, and focuses on assisting or reinforcing shopper decisions.

Figure 8.47 Educational Information Example

Figure 8.48 Interactive Example

Involvement

Involvement motivates increased shopper interaction with your product. It powerfully supports purchase decision-making by drawing shoppers into a meaningful experience with your product. Examples can include a product tester for fragrance or health and beauty products, a free make-up session with cosmetics, or try-me cut-outs in products on-shelf. They can also include more immersive experiences, such as a game trial in an interactive display, a musical instrument try-out room in Best Buy or Guitar Center, or a re-creation of a home environment for a high-end audio and video component trial (see Figure 8.49). The shopper accepts an opportunity to interact with the product and that interaction leads to an increased closure rate.

Figure 8.49 Involvement Examples

Shaping Opportunities

If we revisit the shopping process, we have four significant shaping opportunities to increase our effectiveness and improve our bottom line results. We can get more shoppers to visit our aisle and our section; we can get more people to interact with our item or message; we can convince more people to make an initial purchase; or we can get more people to buy one additional product. The purchase drivers improve results by assisting shoppers at key points in the process. Increased visibility helps interested shoppers see the aisle or section; access to product increases the likelihood of visiting the desired section and can influence the choice of shopping outlet; ease of purchase, education, and involvement each positively influence item interaction while also influencing store selection. All the purchase drivers increase the probability that shoppers will make an initial purchase or add one more item to their shopping basket. As we develop and consider the placement of retail marketing material, it is critical to remember that sales are driven with these five techniques applied from the shopper's perspective (see Figure 8.50).

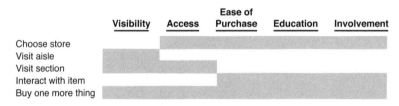

Figure 8.50 Purchase Driver Matrix

Emotional Power

The academic research shows that we all process stimuli on multiple levels simultaneously. Emotion plays a powerful role in motivating purchase, and image size plays a significant part in activating the neuronal activity associated with emotions. The first set of images in Figure 8.51 shows an almost clinical approach to marketing support for the product on-shelf. Compare this with the second image set in Figure 8.52, which utilizes super-sized graphics to communicate the personal payoff we can achieve with use of the featured brands. The first works as a neutral presentation requiring engagement of the cerebral cortex, whereas the second works against the limbic center subconsciously. Emotional connections with brands pay benefits in both immediate sales and long-term brand equity.

Neutral marketing support for products on shelf

Figure 8.51 Neutral Retail Marketing Support

Large graphics featuring payoffs associated with brand use

Figure 8.52 Retail Marketing with Graphic Appeal

Women respond to images that feature relaxation, friendship, and children; men respond to depictions of eroticism, violence, and performance.

The application of a number of these tools is demonstrated in a case study from a regional chain of tire stores that was looking to upgrade its in-store presentation. Initially, the operators had paid little attention to their display of product because they believed they were a 100% assisted sale environment and that the salesperson would guide the shopper through the selection process. As a result, tires were randomly presented on the wall with private label items intermingled with branded offerings and no differentiation between light truck, passenger, or performance tires (see Figure 8.53).

Figure 8.53 Legacy Tire Presentation

Our study of behavior in-store showed that, although all sales were consummated with sales assistance, during peak periods shoppers had browsing time while waiting for salesperson availability. These browsers could not use their time productively and grew impatient with the wait. This lack of self-accessed information was particularly frustrating for nontechnical shoppers. Further, the conversion of sales was hampered by the physical product presentation requiring the shopping group to move randomly across the product display.

The solution involved four elements:

- Segmenting the assortment by category:
  - Light truck
  - Sport
  - Passenger
- Separating brands from private label
- Communicating a defined line structure for private label lines
- Incorporating emotional triggers into the presentation

We repositioned the segments with performance product between passenger and light truck segments. Shoppers who owned either a light truck or passenger car were not interested in tires from the other segment. However, each group could consider a move to more aspirational performance products.

Within each segment, the brands and private label products were aligned in discrete areas. The private label products, which carried higher margins, were broken into a good/better/best line structure and supported with sales material that offered an explanation of the features and benefits each offered. The product and sales support were color-coded so that waiting shoppers could easily make the proper associations in-store.

Emotions were triggered with the product display and graphics. We created new fixtures that implied a sensation of movement by mimicking the position of a tire on the vehicle as it enters a turn. Large, lifestyle graphics were placed above each segment, evoking the safe transport of children for passenger tires, rugged off-road performance for light truck products, and high-speed action for the performance segment. Together, the product orientation on fixture and graphics sought to evoke the emotional connection between shoppers and their chosen vehicle to widen their purchase consideration.

The revised presentation worked against the key objectives of increasing total sales and margin by improving the closure rate and increasing the share for private label tires.

Practical Learnings

In addition to providing insights into human behavior as it applies to the shopping experience, our research and experience led us to develop ten pieces of learning that can be used in the development and execution of retail marketing programs.

Learning One: Distance Delivers Dollars

The amount of money spent in-store is directly related to the time spent in-store and distance covered while in-store. The more areas of the store shoppers visit, the more they will spend.

Learning Two: Shopper Direction Works

Shoppers overwhelmingly follow the shopping path created by retailers. The race track/periphery is visited by 80 percent of shoppers, whereas the traffic in internal aisles generally ranges from 13 to 30 percent.[11] To maximize their efficiency, shoppers routinely walk through the periphery but often leave their carts at the top of internal aisles and then enter to pick up items. Shoppers recall with greater frequency and accuracy the location of items in the periphery, and promotion of one item can stimulate sales of an unrelated but nearby item due to the increased traffic and the shopper's shift from browsing to purchasing mode.

Learning Three: Relaxation Raises Revenue

Shoppers see and process more products and their related retail marketing material when they are not pressed for time. As shoppers mentally slow down and begin to relax, their response to in-store promotions and the level of unplanned purchases increases. The phenomenon can be tracked in a differential response to marketing material by time of day related to an increased openness associated with a general reduction in time pressures and constraints.

Learning Four: Meaningful Cross-Merchandising Works

In-store navigation can be influenced by linking products in meaningful ways. The cross-category benefit is significant for complementary products such as hot dogs/buns or cake mix/frosting. Similarly benefits are also seen from linking products to related events whether it is seasonal (Easter) or an entertainment event (blockbuster movie release).

Learning Five: Beware Information Overload

The amount of information presented in-store has a direct, inverse correlation with the shopper's ability to process and retain that information so that the more data provided, the lower the impact of a particular piece of information. Numerous studies have shown that the amount of time shoppers spend reading marketing at retail messages negatively correlates to their basket size. Marketers must also balance the conclusions made with their messages: Explicit conclusions might minimize confusion but implicit conclusions can increase persuasion as shoppers take more ownership of the essence of the communication (see Figure 8.54).[12]

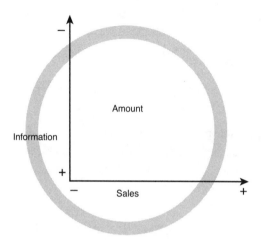

Figure 8.54 Message Balance

Learning Six: List Use Declining

Shoppers' list use continues to decline. The average grocery shopping list has 20 items, with 75 percent of the items defined by category—not brand. When shopping baskets are compared with lists, only 43 percent of purchases were items on the list, indicating that 57 percent of purchases are unplanned for that shopping occasion.

Learning Seven: Context Influences Brand Perception

Brand value perceptions are affected by contextual factors in-store. Proximity or association with prestige brands can enhance the shopper's evaluations for secondary brands; linking small brands with large brands provides a disproportionate percentage lift to the smaller partner. Mixing unrelated products or brands in a single presentation can lead to a lengthier mental processing by the shopper that detracts from brand image and reduces sales for the entire presentation.[13]

Learning Eight: Display Organization Shapes Perception

Display organization influences brand perceptions and the shopper's impression of key purchase consideration attributes. For example, arranging wines by region lifts the importance of this factor in the choice of wine, so that items from prestigious regions increase at the expense of offerings from less prestigious areas.[14]

Learning Nine: Savings Message Impactful

The offering of comparative price information, such as the display of both regular and sale prices, drives sales results by accelerating the shopper's decision-making. It increases shoppers' value perception of the promoted item and decreases the search for additional price information and other data points.

Learning Ten: Marketing at Retail Activity Increases Sales

Properly executed programs increase sales independent of price discounts or other promotional activity. At the same time, marketing at retail activity for one brand can lower the movement of items without marketing support. As we have seen in other areas, overuse of any technique diminishes its effectiveness.[15]

Summary

We began by measuring what shoppers actually do in-store and then understanding why they behave that way by exploring the relevant academic research. By focusing on the steps in the shopping process and the proper application of retail drivers, we can significantly improve bottom-line results.

- Shoppers follow the path that marketers establish for them.

- As they move through the store, they "see" what is meaningful to them on this shopping trip.

- Shoppers reward marketers who minimize their need for mental processing by intuitively anticipating and meeting their shopping needs.

Shoppers punish marketers who require them to think too hard or process too much information in-store.

Endnotes

1. Doug Adams, "POP Measures Up: Learnings from the Supermarket Class of Trade," Washington, D.C.: POPAI (2001), page 14; Doug Adams, "POPAI Convenience Channel Study," (Washington, D.C.: POPAI (2002), page 15; Doug Adams, "POPAI Measuring At-Retail Advertising in Chain Drug Stores," Washington, D.C., POPAI (2004), page 20.

2. "POPAI Mass Merchandising Purchase Study," (1998), http://www.422business.com/html2/articles/199603/marchcon.htm

3. Christoph Haibock, *NeuroMarketing at Retail* (Dubai), 2005.

4. Paco Underhill Interview, 2009.

5. Hugh Phillips, http://www.instore-research.com/Images/PFB_Article_Trends.pdf, *Present and Future of Merchandising*, page 8.

6. Ibid., 8.

7. Hugh Phillips, *The Power of Marketing at Retail*, (Alexandria, VA: POPAI, 2008) page 42.

8. Christoph Haibock, *NeuroMarketing at Retail*, Dubai (2005).

9. Hugh Phillips, *Shopper Psychology*, St. Louis, MO, June (2007).

10. Hugh Phillips, http://www.instore-research.com/Images/Hugh%20PFB%20Presentation1.pdf, *How We Shop*, page 58.

11. Ibid., 39.

12. Ibid., 39.

13. Hugh Phillips, http://www.instore-research.com/Working%20Files/Unilever/Unilever%20Presentation.pdf, page 55.

14. Ibid., 55.

15. Ibid., 58.

9

Online Retailing

Applying Learning and Traditional Tools

In online retailing, shopper behavior follows largely the same patterns as those observed in traditional retail. The lessons from behavioral research remain just as vital, and smart online retailers can equally apply the traditional retailer's tools and success drivers to improve their site's performance. However, e-tailing also possesses several unique characteristics that must be recognized and incorporated into planning. The application of the lessons from traditional retail in a framework that take maximum advantage of the unique online opportunities can help retailers optimize their Internet sales results.

Our review of the impact of behavioral research on shoppers in-store tracked relevant studies across the cognitive, logical, social, and biologic underpinnings of behavior. Just as these areas of study explain shoppers actions in-store, they also provide insight into behavior online. For us, e-tailing extends well beyond the acquisition of goods to encompass the entire world of travel and services, so that anyone with an online presence can benefit from the lessons of the research conducted in-store.

Cognitive Research

The virtual world is even 'more overwhelming than our three-dimensional world. Marketing messages are everywhere, and the shopping options seemingly limitless. We are bombarded with messages at every turn with searches, news reviews, and even email from service providers such as Google. If we did not employ deselection and selective perception to focus on the task at hand, we would never function. However, when we enter a site for shopping, conscious processing assumes a more active role than in-store. Whether we are on Amazon or Craigslist, we have a choice to browse through categories or search for a particular item. Just as we choose our direction in-store, we shape the path we take on our computer screens.

Fatigue remains a critical factor, and the best sites minimize the work that shoppers have to do by structuring their sites using anticipated patterns. In the bricks-and-mortar world, shoppers' expectations vary by type of outlet, and specialty outlets can create an iconoclastic approach for niche segments.

Outside of niche segments, we would posit that the dominant patterns for shopper expectations have been established by Amazon and Apple. Amazon largely shaped shoppers' expectation for online retail by being a first mover and focusing on ease of purchase at every step; Apple established themselves as the leader in intuitive interfaces. As they look for ways to minimize shopper fatigue and frustration, e-tailers would be well served to study the shopping logic employed on these sites to establish architecture for their stores (see Figure 9.1).

Cognitive Factor	Application Online
Deselection	Screening of offers both before and during site visitation
Conscious Processing	Active choice of site navigation
Selective Perception	Seeing what is expected; may miss cues or icons that do not meet expectation
Patterns	Application of subconscious expectations for shopping online

Figure 9.1 Translating Cognitive Behavior

Logical

From a logic viewpoint, the shopping process online is similar to that followed in-store. The difference is that the process is more formal, including a direct opportunity to offer additional items for addition to the shopping basket (see Figure 9.2). As with all retailing, we need to balance the offering of additional items for sale with a risk of exhausting shoppers' patience with the process. Suggestions that have meaning to the shopper will be rewarded; those that are seen as an intrusion will not only result in a lack of response to the offer, but they also may lead to abandonment of the site for other options.

Figure 9.2 Store/Online Parallels

Social

Purchasing online is less of a group activity than shopping in a physical store. Social influencers are important in the shopper's choice of a site to visit, but less so when it comes to navigating the site. The shopping dynamic is an amalgam of conscious and unconscious processes. However, the social forces that shape shopping behavior, as shown as Figure 9.3, affect the choice made prior to the visit much more than those during the visit.

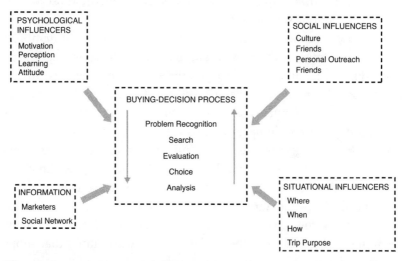

Figure 9.3 Social Forces and Shopping Behavior

However, online shopping affords the opportunity for building powerful virtual communities. These play a vital role in reaffirming your choice of an online retailer and, when used properly, can also drive incremental sales today and tomorrow. These can range from eBay's seller ratings and online communities, to Walmart's offers to connect customers through reviews and online discussion groups, to Amazon's reviews and recommendations from other readers. In each case, the community deepens the involvement of the shopper with the site so that they feel a sense of ownership and belonging.

Biologic

Our response to visual stimulation remains the same in both worlds: Images trigger activity in different parts of our brains, and we can thereby use imagery to promote the desired result. Too often we see e-tailers miss the opportunities afforded by vibrant imagery. At one extreme, we have sites such as Craigslist that are a series of typewritten categories on a white screen. At the other end, we see lifestyle brands such as American Apparel highlighting its products as they are used every day and tapping into aspirational imagery with interactive contests, such as its search for the "best bottom in the world."

Decision Drivers

The decision drivers that lead to e-tail success mirror those within bricks-and-mortar stores, and are detailed in Figure 9.4. The shopper must choose the site, find the category, and then select an item. She must then interact with the item and place it in the shopping basket. With skillful planning and execution, the e-tailer convinces her to add an additional item to the cart and check out. To help the shopper along the way, the online retailer optimizes search results so that the largest number of potential shoppers visit its site. It uses site design and page presentation to trigger the necessary item interaction and position layers of information and interactive elements so that the shopper can chose his own level of immersion in the item experience. The e-tailer presents thoughtful complementary items that the shopper might be open to. These can be a combination of items related by use or interest, or items recommended by like members of the online community that shops this site. Finally, the e-tailer makes the checkout process as quick and painless possible.

Online Decision Steps	Success Drivers
Choose Site	Search Optimization
↓	↓
Choose Category	Site Layout/Navigation
↓	↓
Select Item	Page Layout/Item Presentation
↓	↓
Interact with Item	Item Presentation/Information Options
↓	↓
Place in Shopping Basket	Presentation/Ease of Purchase
↓	↓
Choose Additional Item	Suggested Item Offering
↓	↓
Checkout	Ease of Purchase

Figure 9.4 Decision Steps and Success Drivers

Home Page

Much like the store exterior, the home page works as the shopper's entry point into the online store. It should be clean and inviting and support the brand image. It is critical that you offer opportunities to buy at every turn. Highlight key items, promote bargains, and, most important, if people return for a visit, suggest items that should have interest to them based on their history with you.

The best sites keep track of your history and make suggestions on the item you failed to purchase the last time you visited and related items. These take the form of Amazon's "you viewed this; others who viewed this item also viewed this," eBay's tracking of items you viewed, and Apple's recommendations on potential new purchases based on your most recent purchases. This personalization extends beyond retailing of goods to services, so that the best travel sites remember where you stayed and your previous itineraries so that you can efficiently rebook.

The key for online stores is that the layout fit with expected patterns and that the offerings have meaning to the shopper. Online retailers have a dominant paradigm they can reference in leading sites that have clearly established the expected shopping template. They also have a tremendous edge over bricks-and-mortar stores in that they can personalize their site to specific return shoppers.

Site Navigation

Site navigation is the corollary to store layout. We have seen that the best retailers configure their stores so that they can efficiently serve their shoppers' varying needs, so savvy grocers create layouts allowing shoppers to move through the entire store on their main shopping trip and also efficiently visit the front of the store for a midweek complete meal solution. Likewise, effective e-tailers give shoppers options when they visit their sites so that they can peruse the site in a variety of ways or efficiently search for a single item. If you are a repeat visitor, they give you a shortcut to consummating the purchase you abandoned on the last visit, perhaps reminding you of an intended purchase that was set aside. If the site offers consumable products such as groceries, it keeps track of previous orders or offers the ability to build shopping lists so purchasing entire orders becomes simplified. With proper design, the shopper is empowered, and all the necessary information is at hand so that you can easily finalize a purchase at any point on your visit to the retail site.

Page Design

When the shopper has moved past the home page, the page design is critical. Key elements of the best pages' designs include

- Browsing activity
- Items with meaning to the shopper
- Efficient communication of essential information such as price, size, and so on
- Opportunities to self-select more information to support purchase decision
- Ability to consummate a purchase at any point in the process
- Related items offered for purchase

Let us briefly walk through a typical shopping visit. The shopper visits the site and decides to browse an aisle (for traditional retailers) or a category (for e-tailers). The best sites offer a choice for deeper penetration of the category but also immediately suggest items that might spur immediate purchase activity based either on previous history, timeliness, or special promotion. Once the shopper selects an item, all the necessary information is presented on the page so that the shopper can efficiently compare alternatives in one place. If more information is needed, the shopper can delve deeper into the details. Importantly, at every step, related items are offered for purchase so that the value of the transaction is maximized.

Although these may seem obvious, many e-tailers who get other parts of the equation right miss significant opportunities to optimize purchases as shoppers move through their site. Thus, Safeway presents only a listing of options with no suggested or promoted items offered when you enter an aisle. E-tailers such as Lisa Frank get almost everything wrong by not even including pricing on its page views. This makes it impossible to compare items in the category. The shopper must click on each item to view the price and repeat the process for every offering. The inefficiency is maddening as compared with most sites, and results in tremendous lost opportunities for shoppers who are highly interested in purchasing.

Page Organization

Research firms specializing in eye-tracking studies have established that we view screens in much the same way we view our three-dimensional world.[1] Whether we are watching a television screen or a computer monitor, our eyes find the object of interest and then move around that item to take in other items in the area. Our behavior on the screen is similar to that measured by Dr. Hugh Phillips in-store.[2] Design is the key to focusing attention so that the page view results in a sale. Much as retailers use clean lines and bookending to focus attention, strong e-tailers design their pages so the attention is focused, and shoppers do not wander down a series of options that overload the senses and lead to an abandonment of the site without making a purchase. At the same time, pages should not be too pristine, or you will miss the opportunity to create a related sale.

Purchase Drivers

The essential elements involved in deciding to purchase are the same whether the sale is consummated online or in a three-dimensional retail environment. Consequently, the purchase drivers (visibility, access, ease of purchase, communication/education, and involvement) are vitally important to optimizing results. The application of these drivers requires adjustments in strategy and takes a slightly different expression to increasing sales.

Visibility

Online visibility relates to our ability to see items and their marketing message onscreen. As shoppers orient themselves upon entering a store, they also orient themselves on an e-tailer's home page. What they see is directly related to the relevance the offerings have to them on this visit. Contrasting the online store with traditional retail, retailers can better influence the path of shopper traffic in-store but must generally position items that will pass within view against identified shopper segments; e-tailers can more precisely target the items shown to the shopper based on previous visits and the shopper's activity on this visit. As e-tailers increase their knowledge of what is driving the shopper's visit, they have the opportunity to increase the relevance of the items presented so that visibility can be greatly enhanced (see Figure 9.5).

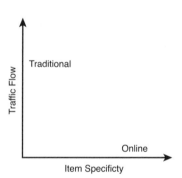

Figure 9.5 Product Exposure Comparison

Access

Access online is driven by the relative exposure of the product to shoppers. Obviously an item such as the Kindle, which is the dominant

---

feature on Amazon's home page, has a much greater product access than a branded electronic item found only through a shopper-directed search. Likewise, a new release from a best-selling author bannered on all book searches will have much greater product access than individual book titles from the catalog that appear only when requested. The greater the exposure or access to the product, the higher the sales will be, as a portion of the shoppers to whom the item is presented will find relevance in the offering and make a purchase. For e-tailers, sales are maximized when product access closely correlates to relevance to the shopper (see Figure 9.6).

Figure 9.6 Access and Relevance Impact

Ease of Purchase

As we saw in-store, the easier it is to make a purchase, the more shoppers will buy. Online ease of purchase takes various forms:

- Reminding shoppers of the items they viewed on their last visit

- Suggesting items of similar interest to the previous items purchased

- Intuitively recommending items based on current searches

- Suggesting intelligent add-on items

- Making it easy to repeat consumable purchases (stored lists, preferences, or itineraries)

- Relevant responses to searches

- A quick path to purchase finalization after a choice is made

Incomplete information, a tedious order consummation process, and irrelevant search results lead to frustration. The bar for intuitive responses and ease of use at every step of the process creates a high level of expectation for all e-tailers.

Communication/Education

The research in-store shows us that education is a tool that must be applied with great precision. Complex categories respond positively to a depth of information, but sales can decrease as the amount of information grows and shoppers become overwhelmed. In retail stores, the marketer must make an educated choice about the amount of data to be presented and carefully gauge shopper responses to find a general sweet spot.

The online world offers a relatively simple path to optimizing communication. Savvy online merchants present the product simply so that those who know what they want or do not want to be confused with too much information have a clear path to purchase. At the same time, they offer a "more info" option so that those who are unsure can gather additional details. The best merchants extend the discussion to their online communities so that group feedback can provide a third-party validation and added assurance to those contemplating a purchase. The technique works for books and technical purchases, and the capability to layer information gives online retailers the opportunity to have shoppers customize the amount of information they need.

Involvement

Although online stores cannot replicate the experience of a tactile interaction with the product offered for sale, they have multiple opportunities for shoppers to get involved with offerings. Involvement techniques include samples of books or music, videos of products in use, and introductions to online communities of users and reviewers. For nonmerchandise offerings such as travel, sites can offer the opportunity to view the property, virtually tour the room, or get excited about sights in the area. The key for involvement is that it has meaning for the shopper, and the multiple pathways offered through intelligent web design provide the shopper with a choice of the level and type of involvement that will have meaning.

Managing Online Dynamics

The principles of good retailing and tools for optimizing the shopping experience apply in three-dimensional and online stores. Each environment has unique opportunities and limitations, and the best practitioners find ways to maximize their opportunities. Online retailers cede control of the navigation after their home page to shoppers. They can influence navigation in their careful introduction to the shopping experience. They have tremendous opportunity to make the items they present relevant by reacting to previous searches and the shoppers' activity during their visit.

Site volume is a function of the total transactions that result in a sale and the size of the shopping basket. These are influenced by the ease of purchase and the relevance of the items presented to shoppers during their visit. Online winners make their transaction easy to complete on each visit and leverage the information provided by the shopper to increase the number of items selected for purchase (see Figure 9.7).

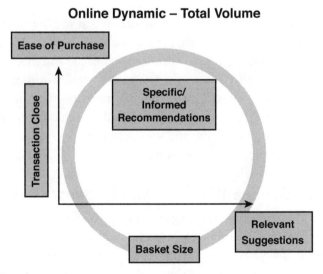

Figure 9.7 Online Volume Dynamic

Online Tools

Applying the lessons from the research in retail stores online leads us to ten tools for increasing online success.

Tool #1—Optimize Search and Existing Points of Contact

Before shoppers can buy from your site, they need to find it. If you are a giant of online retailing, shoppers are aware of your offering and will find you. Online merchants with a presence in the traditional retail world need to have a clear strategy for what they want to accomplish online and then maximize every contact point to drive shoppers onto their online sites. Online retailing will never replace brick-and-mortar. However, online sales are an important part of total sales activity, and their share of sales will continue to grow. Using existing interactions with consumers to drive visits online builds brand preference and can ensure that you retain customers and grow your share of their total spending.

For all merchants selling online, it is important that you optimize search. Consumers who use a search engine are qualified customers. You need to work to make sure that your store appears in the search so that you get consideration and visits. In the traditional retail world, new shoppers find your store by walking through a mall or a shopping district and noticing your exterior. In the online world, search is the counterpart to the stroll through the mall, and you need to make sure that you are presented where shoppers are looking.

Tool #2—Operate Within Dominant Shopper Patterns

Shoppers use shortcuts and unconsciously reference patterns when shopping online just as they do in traditional stores. By incorporating the patterns associated with the dominant online retailers, you support the unconscious expectation of shoppers and make your site seem easier to use and more intuitive to navigate. This comfort with the shopping environment promotes greater relaxation that encourages the shopper to linger and increases the number of items that are considered for inclusion in the shopping basket. By contrast, introducing a new navigation pattern causes shoppers to think about what they are doing at each step and can lead to fatigue and a potential abandonment of the first purchase without even considering secondary items.

Tool #3—Make the Site Meaningful to Shoppers

If your site is a means of purchasing a desired product, shoppers will visit, buy the single item, and leave. This scenario delivers a measure of volume but does not optimize the opportunity the medium offers.

Shoppers are considering a purchase because it relates to something of interest and meaning to them. As food relates to cooking, song downloads to music, and hotel rooms to travel, shoppers online are fulfilling a need that is part of a larger interest. The more you can make your site meaningful to that larger interest, the more of their purchases you will earn, so that you become the preferred site for that area of interest.

Tool #4—Implement a Multiplatform Strategy

When you have presence in the traditional and online worlds, look for ways to make each presence reinforce the other. Executed properly, the online experience makes the store visit easier and more rewarding, whereas the store visit drives shoppers online as a way to extend the store and increase the role the website plays within that area of interest for shoppers.

Apple executes this strategy well as it encourages shoppers to register certain store activities online and even have them work on a computer in-store if they failed to preregister. Thus appointments at the Genius Bar are scheduled online. If you want to buy an iPhone, you enter the necessary information online. If you do this from home, the process is fast; if you do not, an associate helps you complete the process on a computer. The result is that the physical store and the online presence are linked, visitation to the site is encouraged, and you quickly learn that the online presence is an extension of the store to be visited before a planned trip.

Tool #5—Personalize Your Offerings

Relevancy drives response. Traditional retailers need to focus their offerings on an identified group of shoppers to maximize relevancy. Online merchants can focus the offering on a unique individual. Smart e-tailers incorporate past visits and purchases into their recommendation. The best refine their recommendations based on current site visits.

Tool #6—Motivate Desired Behavior

All retailers make more money with a larger shopping basket. But most online merchants face an additional hurdle associated with the direct marketing model. Direct marketers have a relatively fixed cost to pack, process, and ship an order, so that an order for a single $10 item is most likely unprofitable, whereas an order for ten of the same item totaling $100 will be highly profitable. Shoppers need to factor the delivery charge into their acquisition cost. As handling and shipping costs are spread over multiple items, their impact diminishes, and the order becomes more profitable for the merchant with a lower per-item delivery cost for the shoppers.

Although the break-even point varies dramatically across different merchants, the best merchants understand the profit dynamics associated with building an order and incorporate incentives into their offerings so that shoppers become willing partners in building the merchant's profitability.

Poor operators, such as Lisa Frank, remain mute on order size and leave shoppers to find their own way through their online stores. With a low average ticket per item, shoppers are surprised by the weight of the delivery charges and will abandon their shopping basket or be frustrated with the experience and less likely to return.

By contrast, smart operators, such as the Oriental Trading Company, sell merchandise with roughly the same average price but offer incentives to their shoppers to earn free shipping by building their order to defined dollar levels. Shoppers know what the shipping charge is likely to be up front and factor that into their shopping behavior as they browse the site. The result is an average order size above the industry average that fulfills the merchant's goals and satisfies the shoppers in achieving a total order target size they set.

Tool #7—Analyze Data

Merchants online possess unprecedented levels of data on shoppers' behavior when they visit their sites. They can leverage that data to understand where shoppers abandon their purchases and when shoppers respond to offers. They can test alternative scenarios in real time and measure responses. By leveraging the malleability of the medium and the granular data available, they can gain greater understanding of their shoppers' behavior online so that they can identify offers and techniques that optimize close rates and the frequency with which secondary items are added to the order.

Tool #8—Layer Your Information and Immersion

Traditional retailers have to navigate a treacherous strait in determining the amount of information to be offered on shelf. Take advantage of the flexibility the Internet offers by keeping the information simple on the initial page and then positioning layers of involvement and immersion behind this offering. If shoppers just want to verify that the book is the one they are seeking by looking at the cover, let them simply make their purchase at this point. If the shopper wants to consider the book by looking through the chapters and seeing what other people said about the book, give them that opportunity as an option. If the shopper is interested in the topic and not sure of which book to purchase, support her search by suggesting related titles. This approach, favored by Amazon, lets shoppers choose their level of involvement and supports the predominant shopping patterns for books.

A contrasting approach would be to list all the technical information associated with a computer on the initial page offering. This technique unnecessarily reflects a traditional retail decision in which your choice on information is static. This approach can overwhelm the casual shopper and lead to indecision that causes her to abandon your site. A better approach is to replicate the Amazon book offering with a simple benefits presentation that is fast with sharp pictures, and so on. For shoppers who want more information, you can offer opportunities to view technical data, reviews, evaluate alternatives, and so on.

The online store is a flexible medium. The best online merchants use that flexibility so that shoppers easily get the experience that is most relevant to them.

Tool #9—Connect and Involve

After you connect with your shoppers, connect them with each other to deepen the relationship with your site. Look for opportunities to create communities of shoppers so that you create a connection that extends beyond the goods and services offered. Examples range from eBay, which was an early mover in creating communities, to Walmart, which hosts discussion groups around broad topics for young families and posts a series of blogs. Understand the areas of interest to your shoppers and create reasons for them to use your site as a portal to their interests so that you have additional contact points.

Tool #10—Leverage the Path to Purchase

With greater precision than traditional retail, online shoppers follow a defined path to purchase. Look for opportunities to recommend a relevant additional item at each step along that journey. The worst practitioners approach the shopping process clinically. When you enter a category, they will list an option in script to one side with no visuals, or provide only the information that is necessary to assist with your navigation to the next page. Mid-level performers offer purchase selections in addition to the navigation tools, but do not take advantage of the entire page. The best sites combine navigation tools with personalized suggestions, timely suggestions, and top sellers. To avoid overload, they clearly define the sections and keep them consistent throughout all the categories offered.

The optimal page design, as shown in Figure 9.8, approaches the page in quadrants, with navigation tools on the left, timely offerings in the upper middle, personalized selections in the bottom middle, and best-sellers on the right. Too often retailers miss the opportunity to suggest additional items by not leveraging one of these quadrants.

After the decision to purchase has been made, suggest related items before taking the shopper to the checkout page. While at the checkout page, offer one more opportunity to build the order.

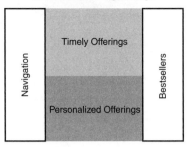

Recommended Page Design

Figure 9.8 Recommended Page Design

Endnotes

1. Hugh Phillips, "The Power of Marketing at Retail," Alexandria, VA, POPAI (2008), pages 41-43.

2. Ibid., 37-39.

10

Measuring Return on Investment

Delivering Results

Dynamic Tensions

Retail marketing is an art and a science. The scientific part of the equation includes segmenting and analyzing shoppers, defining performance drivers, and composing precise mathematical equations that measure and predict performance. The art comes into play in implementing those strategies so that they deliver the desired results.

Retail campaign optimization requires the careful navigation of a series of dynamic tensions that require careful strategy development. These dynamic tensions are double-edged swords—an overly conservative approach limits the number of shoppers visiting our stores or sections and suboptimizes the value of the traffic we generate; an overly aggressive implementation likewise restricts traffic and constrains the size of the potential shopping basket. We need to recognize and understand these tensions to properly balance our program planning.

The tensions begin with our modern shopper. Although she is unbelievably empowered with access to information and products unimaginable a few years ago, the price of this empowerment is overload. However, the intrusion of media and uninterrupted access to work and family results in a loss of personal time and increased stress levels (see Figure 10.1).

Consumer Dynamic

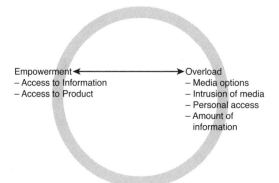

Empowerment ←——————————→ Overload
– Access to Information   – Media options
– Access to Product   – Intrusion of media
                                                 – Personal access
                                                 – Amount of
                                                    information

Figure 10.1 Consumer Dynamic

Within the retail environment, store layout represents a significant point of strategic tension affecting shopper navigation (see Figure 10.2). We know that sales are linked to the distance traveled in store. However, traffic into the store is influenced by convenience. Although we want to maximize the areas of the store visited for those shoppers engaged in a main shopping trip that requires them to visit the entire store, we also want to deliver sufficient convenience for fill-in trips so that we attract the maximum number of visits. We want to make our store the best option for shoppers completing their personal value equations and calculating the likely effort required to complete their mission. Strategically, location of sections within the store and adjacencies are the tools we can employ to optimize the value to our targeted shoppers.

The second retail challenge involves assortment; we need to balance the convenience of providing many categories against the depth of product choices required to sustain credibility as a preferred destination. The tension in assortment is exacerbated by the desire to generate sufficient SKU productivity to support net profit objectives (see Figure 10.3). The old general store pursued a philosophy of broad categories and narrow item options because it was required to meet the broad needs of its community, and shoppers lived with minimal shopping options. Today, the middle ground is a no man's land of mediocrity on a path to extinction. Success comes on the peripheries, with successful strategies including

- Narrow category presentation and a deep level of item choices; that is, category specialists such as an REI

- Broad product assortments with narrow product offerings, such as deep discounters like Aldi and warehouse clubs

- Broad categories with deep offerings, such as hypermarkets and supercenters

Retail Dynamic – Navigation

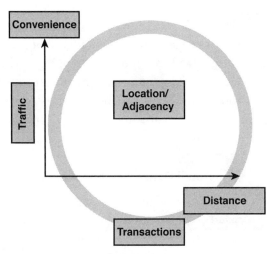

Figure 10.2 Retail Dynamic-Navigation

Retail Dynamic–Assortment

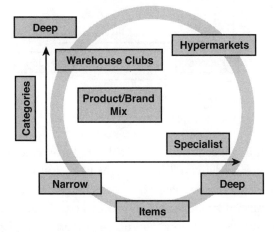

Figure 10.3 Retail Dynamic-Assortment

Familiarity is an often overlooked part of retail strategy. The easier we make the shopping experience for shoppers, the more relaxed they will be and the more messages they will see. By extension, the more difficult we make the task, the more fatigued they become, purchasing fewer items. However, we know that shoppers will expend the minimal effort to achieve their objective and, if a store is overly familiar, they will complete their mission on autopilot, editing out thousands of potential stimuli. The result is a shopping basket that has fewer items than it could.

Comfort with a store breeds loyalty and repeat visits. Disruption creates fatigue during the visits and leads to a loss of total shoppers. The proper amount of dissonance introduced into the shopping environment will not fatigue shippers and will intrude on their comfort zone just enough to cause them to notice more items and increase the size of the shopping basket (see Figure 10.4). If the dissonant messages have value to shoppers, they will reward marketers with vastly improved results.

Retail Dynamic – Familiarity

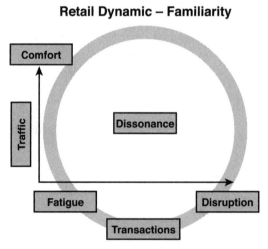

Figure 10.4 Retail Dynamic-Familiarity

A final tension involves the messages delivered in-store. We know that the proper message delivered in the right place improves results (see Figure 10.5). However, we have to intelligently manage our choice of emotional versus informational messages as a part of our total communication to shoppers. We know that making messages implicit increases their power as shoppers draw their own conclusions, but explicit messages are clearer and minimize confusion. Likewise, complex products require detailed explanation, but the introduction of a number of points to consider decreases our persuasion and conversion as the amount of information offered in store inversely mirrors the sales impact of the information presented.

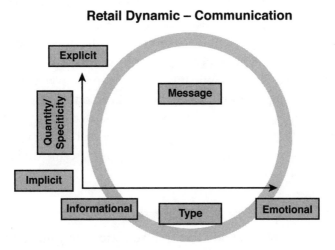

Retail Dynamic – Communication

Figure 10.5 Retail Dynamic-Communication

Retail Tools

Our review of the relevant research and a process for developing and implementing strategies leads us to the proposal of ten tools for increasing retail success.

Tool #1—Make a Stand

Trying to be all things to all shoppers is a certain path to failure. Success today and tomorrow will be driven by an identification of the shoppers who are important to you, an understanding of what is important to them, the development of a meaningful brand promise, and the consistent delivery against that promise. Segment the shopper universe, define your market to be served, and work a formal process to attain and maintain intimacy with them (see Figure 10.6).

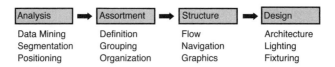

Analysis	Assortment	Structure	Design
Data Mining	Definition	Flow	Architecture
Segmentation	Grouping	Navigation	Lighting
Positioning	Organization	Graphics	Fixturing

Figure 10.6 Retail Definition Elements

Tool #2—Operate Within Dominant Shopper Schemata

Understand shoppers' necessary use of shortcuts, and position your products and messages so they are familiar yet also appropriately interruptive in a manner that is meaningful to the shoppers you target. Work with, and through, the dominant organizing principles employed by your target shoppers in both the physical positioning of product and marketing support and the messages communicated. Strategically, consider the application of all the tools at your disposal against the targeted shopper groups: store entrance, layout, navigation, segment adjacencies, and planograms.

Tool #3—Structure Meaningful Conversations

Approach the time shoppers spend in your store, in your section, and with your brand as a conversation. Understanding what is important to the shoppers you serve in this location, make that conversation meaningful by controlling the amount of information and delivering the desired information in that place at that particular time. Make connections for the shoppers and assist them in their mission to reap the rewards of trial, loyalty, and greater sales.

Tool #4—Use Complementary Merchandising

Part of making connections for shoppers includes an anticipation of related needs. At times the relationship is easily seen and flows from the logical combination of items generally required for a complete experience, as with our examples of hot dogs and buns or cake mix and frosting. At other times, the connections may be mood, occasion, or need-state based. Examples include wine with steak or seafood, beer with brats, or even beer with diapers. Making connections for shoppers, either explicitly or implicitly, increases sales when the connection has meaning to the shopper.

Tool #5—Focus Attention

After shoppers locate an item or area of interest, they are not inclined to remain focused. Instead, their attention wanders, and other potential items of interest enter their field of vision. We can leverage this peripheral exploration with complementary merchandising and intuitive adjacencies, but first we must make sure that we convert their interest into a transaction. To do so we need to make certain that we

- Strategically use signposts to attract shoppers.

- Define the section so that the area for consideration is intuitively understood and we hold the shoppers' attention.

- Edit the assortment so that the options to be considered make sense and do not overwhelm shoppers, resulting in fatigue or confusion that leads to a decision postponement.

- Present the product choices in a clean planogram that appeals to shoppers, subconsciously and consciously, as attractive and easy to shop.

- Support the product presentation with the marketing at retail messages and tools that appropriately assist shoppers in their decision making.

Tool #6—Use Adjacencies

Shoppers are on a mission during which they screen out nonessential products until they locate a product or message of interest. We must leverage the period in which they shift from browsing/macroscan activity to purchase consideration to first close the sale and then trigger the consideration of additional items. We can use the positioning of related categories adjacent to, or in proximity with, the item of focus to reduce shoppers' workload. Traffic is a precious commodity, and we need to optimize the value of shopper traffic to create incremental sales by maximizing the value of purchase decision points.

Tool #7—Leverage Brands

Brands have tremendous power. Marketers have spent billions of dollars making implicit and explicit connections between consumer aspirations and their products so that they become powerful shortcuts for shoppers and often define a category. Brand power includes trade dress and the powerful imagery with which they have drawn associations. Brands can

- Influence the choice of channel or retailer
- Draw traffic to an area of the store
- Define a section or category
- Provide additional shopper insight through their extensive research that yields a deep understanding of their consumers
- Increase movement of secondary brands/products
- Deliver emotional power

Tool #8—Choose When to Interrupt Traffic Flow

Our shopping environments need to be comfortable and efficient to attract shoppers and minimize the fatigue that can depress sales. However, we need to protect against the potential for shoppers to move through the stores on automatic pilot mechanically picking up the items on their mental list and never "seeing" anything else. The key is to control the flow and pace of traffic.

First, create spaces to linger so that shoppers are encouraged to mentally slow down, increasing their relaxation that, in turn, enhances their receptivity to more of the stimuli presented in store. Then, create additional opportunities to see and interact with products by selectively interrupting traffic flow in a manner that has meaning to your shoppers.

Tool #9—Execute Consistently

Today's shoppers move freely across channels and choose widely divergent levels of service and assortment as they seek to complete their shopping needs. An essential factor in their choice of outlet is the consistency of the actual experience with their expectations. Controlled dissonance can increase results by creatively intruding on the shoppers' consciousness to deliver a message of value. Too much incongruity in the shopping environment requires conscious mental processing that will quickly lead to fatigue and abandonment of the shopping trip. We need to deliver consistently through all levels of design and execution to support the targeted shoppers' expectations.

Tool #10—Measure and Refine

As intelligent and brilliantly designed and executed as our program may be, it is absolutely essential that we consistently drive our learning and expectations through all the involved levels of our organizations and then measure our results so that we can identify anomalies and improve future results. First, we must create integrated teams so that we draw on all the knowledge available to us to build programs, and then we must share the consolidated learning back throughout our teams. We must establish key metrics and goals for our programs and measure our results with an accompanying interdisciplinary review to discuss successes and failures and identify opportunity areas for future programs. We operate in a period of an ever-increasing pace of change, so we need to constantly refine and enhance our strategy and tactics.

Return on Investment Models

Return on investment (ROI) is critical to the long-term success of our programs and plays a crucial role by establishing the metrics that drive measurement and refinement. On the surface, calculating ROI is a simple matter of measuring direct costs against the direct benefits generated:

$$\frac{\text{Incremental profit on item sales}}{\text{Vehicle cost}}$$

However, multiple levels of measurement complexity exist, depending on

- Participant viewpoint
- Perspective on total returns
- Level of cost measured

Traditional Model

A traditional return on investment model calculation looks something like this:

**Brand A: ROI Calculation for
Free-Standing Display**

Base sales	$3,000 (A)
Lift	33% (B)
Incremental sales	$996 (C = A × B)
Variable profit	28% (D)
Incremental profit	$279 (E = C × D)
Display cost	$150 (F)
Net profit	$129 (G = E − F)
ROI	85.9% (H = (G/E) × 100)
M@R cost per incremental sales dollar	15.1% (I = F / C)

Expansive Model

Although it is important to understand direct costs and returns, our previous discussions have conclusively shown that retail marketing delivers meaningful benefits well beyond the incremental sales generated during a specific period of time. The POPAI MARI subcommittee expanded the consideration of the total benefits that could be associated with retail marketing efforts (see Figure 10.7) to include[1]

- Incremental sales
- Incremental profits
- Total market basket impact
- Brand impact
- Choice of manufacturer
- Category impact
- Choice of store
- Channel selection

Potential Benefits

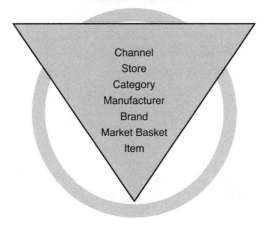

Channel
Store
Category
Manufacturer
Brand
Market Basket
Item

Figure 10.7 Potential Benefits

Likewise, the potential costs associated with marketing at retail campaigns extend beyond the direct costs of the material itself (see Figure 10.8) and can include[2]

- Cost of vehicle

- Cost of goods to support display

- Setup costs

- Disposal cost

- Opportunity cost for space utilized

- Trade allowances

- Distribution cost

Potential Costs

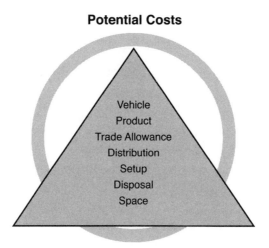

Figure 10.8 Potential Costs

Considering this more robust view of the total costs and returns generated by retail marketing efforts (see Figure 10.9), we end up with this measurement model:

$$\frac{\text{Potential Benefits}}{\text{Potential Costs}}$$

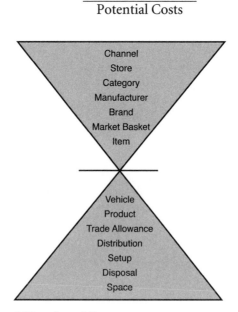

Figure 10.9 Potential Benefits and Costs

Using these considerations we can mathematically express the ROI from a variety of participant viewpoints, and as either a post-program evaluation tool or a preprogram predictor.

Overall Evaluation Model

The overall evaluation model in Figure 10.10 incorporates all the potential benefits and costs that could be associated with a program for both brands and retailers. The potential benefits include direct sales and the broader, long-term benefits; the cost considerations include direct investments in the marketing at retail activity and the opportunity cost associated with the use of retail space.[3]

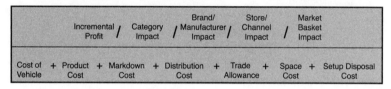

Figure 10.10 Retail Marketing ROI Model

Analytic Retail Model

The analytic models look back to measure the return generated from recently concluded marketing efforts. In the retail model shown in Figure 10.11, we consider the direct and indirect retailer costs and benefits so that we remove the consideration of manufacturer choice and trade allowance costs.[4]

		Store/	
Incremental Profit	/ Category Impact	/ Channel Impact	/ Total Market Basket Impact

| Cost of Vehicle | + | Product Cost | + | Markdown Cost | + | Distribution Cost | + | Space Cost | + | Setup Disposal Cost |

Figure 10.11 Retail Marketing Retailer ROI Model Without Compliance

Analytic Brand Model

In the analytic brand model in Figure 10.12, we remove considerations of the benefits associated with total market basket size and store/channel selections and those costs which do not accrue to brands, such as opportunity cost consumed by the space devoted to the marketing effort. In developing separate measures for brands and retailers, it is not that the retailer concerns are not important to brands and brands scorecards are not important to retailers. Rather, it is important to have a clear measure of the returns our efforts generate against our own financial report cards.[5]

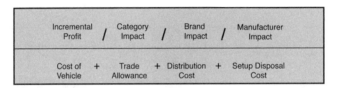

Figure 10.12 Retail Marketing Brand ROI Model

Retail Model

Our predictive models look forward to forecast expected results for proposed marketing programs based on our experience and analyses of previous programs. The overall predictive model in Figure 10.13 introduces the consideration of the expected level of field implementation for the campaign (compliance). All our anticipated benefits are modified by the percentage of displays actually executed in store. On the cost side, all our costs remain except those related to setup and opportunity costs. The completion of predictive models in concert with program development can establish important markers for evaluating the success of programs at their conclusion.[6]

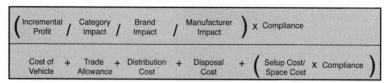

Figure 10.13 Retail Marketing Retailer ROI Model with Compliance

Achieving Success Through Shopper Intimacy

Profound changes are shaking our retail world. These changes are driven by a combination of macro societal changes in shopper composition, attitude, and empowerment, the implosion of traditional media models, and tectonic shifts in the retail landscape. Concurrent with these macro changes, an explosion of research into shoppers' behavior at retail has produced and continues to generate a tremendous number of insights that dramatically raise the level of available knowledge. This increased knowledge has implications for all retail marketing participants. For thought leaders, the research opens significant new opportunities for unlocking increased growth and profits, whereas a failure to properly employ the data will leave others with outdated models that deliver declining returns.

Today's winners recognize the opportunities that the market changes and new information provide, and they build programs that position themselves for sustained growth by implementing a process that routinely translates their data into shopper intimacy and then drives this knowledge throughout their organizations. They create a cycle in which they analyze data to develop the insights that inform a targeted, shopper-focused strategy that incorporates the key objectives of all participants. Their strategy is then implemented with subsequent measurement and analyses of the results in a search for additional insights that will improve future plans.

This virtuous cycle of regularly translating new information into actions and analyses that culminates in intimacy is centered on the optimization of retail space productivity and the effectiveness of marketing budgets, as shown in Figure 10.14. Shopper intimacy ultimately drives the key decisions we make about whom we target, the tools we employ to reach them (what), when we seek to engage them, and the messages we utilize (how).[7]

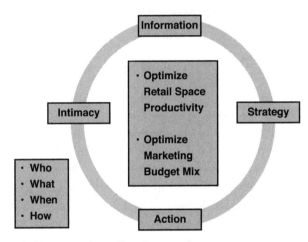

Figure 10.14 Retail Marketing Effectiveness Cycle

Optimization of retail performance depends on the achievement of shopper intimacy developed and implemented in a collaborative process that unites the key participants in the pursuit of shared goals (see Figure 10.15). Each participant must direct their efforts on servicing a particular shopper and meeting her needs in a particular place. By bringing their unique insights together, brands, retailers, and agencies increase the value of their analyses. By understanding the needs of each constituency and appreciating the points of convergence and divergence, participants increase the quality of their strategies and the level of implementation for their programs.

Figure 10.15 Integration and Collaboration

Although the benefits of this knowledge-based, integrated approach are immense, the level of change for participants in retail marketing and their organizations is massive. The development of the store as a medium will lead to increased awareness of retail marketing and spur greater innovation that will, in turn, stimulate the development of new vehicles while increasing the premium for insight and creativity. Greater agency involvement will accompany a shift of media dollars into the retail arena with the underwriters demanding accountability and reliable metrics. Increased collaboration and the inclusion of new players in the planning mix will lead to a redefinition of roles, the development of a common language, and eventual agreement on general principles and methodologies.

Retailers will face difficult decisions on the allocation and use of space that will affect assortment choices. Demand will grow for reliable compliance reporting for planned programs. Brands will reallocate their marketing dollars and merchandising roles will change dramatically as the focus of retail presentation grows to include a broader spectrum of brand communication goals. Agencies will heighten their involvement as discussions become increasingly strategic with an expanding search for innovation.

As practitioners grow in sophistication, they will resolve the organizational tensions in the current structures that arise from divergent focal points by concentrating on the mutual gains that accrue to the teams that direct their attention on shoppers' needs.

Organizational Tensions

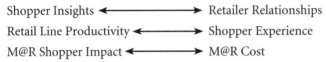

The end result will be a deeper understanding of shoppers in retail stores and increased space productivity as we collectively do a better job of anticipating and meeting shoppers' needs. As information and understanding become increasingly available, we increase the opportunity to improve returns by applying greater efficiency throughout the process of reaching and servicing consumers and shoppers. Internally, our dialogue becomes increasingly strategic as a prelude to a similar elevation of the discourse that expands to include all key participants.

The process detailed in Figure 10.16 begins with an acknowledgment and acceptance of the changed environment in which we now operate. This acceptance leads to an aggressive search for data that we can translate into insights that inform our development of targeted strategies and action plans that include all the key stakeholders. We then gather the resources needed to implement the plan and analyze our results against the key metrics established for our program to unlock new insights that lead us to an intimacy with the shoppers we target. The integration of process and data in an inclusive cycle of continuous testing and refinement will drive consistent improvements in sales and productivity.

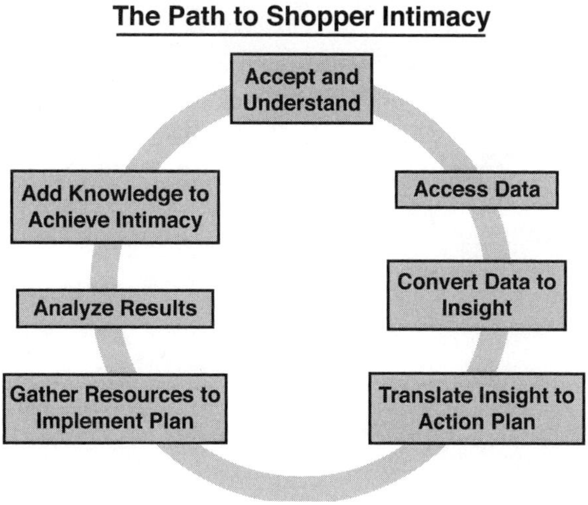

The Path to Shopper Intimacy

Figure 10.16 The Path to Shopper Intimacy

Endnotes

1. Authors' notes (December 2006).

2. Ibid.

3. Ibid.

4. Ibid.

4. Ibid.

5. Ibid.

6. Ibid.

7. Ibid.

Index

A

access, 183
accumulation rules for media measures, 80
accuracy of measurements, 36-37
actual audience reach, 82
Adaptation level theory, 137
adjacencies, 165-168, 221
Ahold USA, 93
aisle sensors, 91
Albertsons, 91
Aldi, 164
aligning store shelves, 179-180
American Research Federation (ARF), 79
amount of retail marketing, 53-55
analysis
  in REAP, 8
  shopper analysis integration
    explained, 12-14
    retail marketing scorecards, 14-15
    segmentation premiums, 15-16
    traditional shopper segmentation traits,
    16-17
analytic brand model (ROI), 228
analytic retail model (ROI), 227
Anheuser-Busch, 103
A&P, 93
Apple Store, 154
ARF (American Research Federation), 79
assisted versus open sell, 184
assortment, 8, 163-164, 216-217
attention, focusing, 221
audience
  audience delivery worksheet, 84-85
  defined, 80
  size of, 94

B

behavior. *See* shopper behavior
Best Buy, 152
best practices model, 122
biologic, 141-143, 200
Blackwell, Roger, 131
boredom, 141
brand acceptance scorecard, 15
brand A message impact ratio (MARI), 113

brands
  brand channel segmentation, 19
  brand-focused messages, 70-71
  brand ROI measurement, 38
  dominant brand on lowest shelf, 172
  dominant brand side by side, 173
  leveraging, 221-222
  value perceptions, 193
British Petroleum, 103
Brooks. *See* drug store study

C

Calhoun, David, 94
Carrefour, 152
case studies (REAP)
  brand channel segmentation, 19
  collaborative failure, 18-19
  retailer assortment rationalization, 17-18
  shopper psychographic segmentation,
    20-23
Catapult Marketing, 93
category sales response to price/sales
    messaging, 68
category shopping variations within stores,
    35-36
Chabris, Christopher, 127
chain drug store study. *See* drug store study
Chanel, 155
channel segmentation, 19
channel studies
  convenience store study, 43-59
  drug store study, 63-78
  supermarket study, 26-40
    actual audience reach, 82
    IRP (In-Store Rating Points), 82-83
    potential reach, 81
choosing when to interrupt traffic flow, 222
Christian Dior, 155
ClipCam technology, 105
Clorox, 93
close rates by category, 95
close rates by channel, 95
Coca-Cola, 91, 103
cognitive research, 126, 197-198
  conscious processing, 128-129
  consistency, 131-134
  deselection, 127-128

pattern and structures, 129-131
    selective perception, 129
collaboration, 231
collaborative failure, 18-19
color palette, 154-156
complementary merchandising, 220
communication, 206, 218-219
comparative price information, 194
compare and save effectiveness ratio, 72-73
ConAgra Foods, 93
connecting with shoppers in online
    retailing, 212
conscious processing, 128-129
consistency, 131-134, 141
    consistent execution, 222
    consistent marketing performance areas, 33
constituency inclusion (REAP), 9-12
consumer behavior. *See* shopper behavior
contemporary supermarket layout, 159-160
context, 193
convenience store study (POPAI)
    amount of retail marketing, 53-55
    average brand lift by category, 48
    average coverage by brand category, 45
    core area versus outdoor placement, 50-51
    cost efficiency, 57-58
    custom versus generic sales increase, 53
    effectiveness ratio impact, 55-56
    key retail marketing location, 46
    marketing messages, 48-49
    outdoor versus indoor lift, 51-52
    overview, 43-44
    percentage of category retail marketing by
        location, 47
    proof of placement, 56-57
    range of sales life, 49-50
    retail marketing placement, 45
    retail marketing techniques, 47
    sales effectiveness, 57-58
    small brand relative sales increase, 52-53
    success element importance by segment,
        58-59
conversion metrics, 108-109
core area placement, 50-51
cost efficiency, 57-58
cost per thousand (CPM), 75-77, 79, 83-84
cross-merchandising, 182, 192
custom sales increase, 53
CVS. *See* drug store study

D

data analysis in online retailing, 211
decision drivers, 200-201. *See also* purchase
    drivers; retail success drivers
    emotional power, 188-191
    financial impact of presentation
        optimization, 145-146
    leveraging related items, 177-180
    planned versus unplanned purchases,
        148-150

retail factors and purchase decision
    types, 145
retail success dynamic, 146-148
shaping opportunities, 187-188
tips and guidelines, 191-194
demographic shifts, 2
deselection, 127-128
design
    home pages, 202-203
    in REAP, 9
Diageo, 103
differential close rates by category, 95
differential close rates by channel, 95
DigiTrack software, 105
discourse shift, 121
display organization, 194
dominant brand on lowest shelf, 172
dominant brand side by side, 173
dominant shopper patterns, 208-209, 220
drug store layout, 158
drug store study (POPAI)
    brand-focused messages, 70-71
    category sales response to price/sales
        messaging, 68
    compare and save effectiveness ratio, 72-73
    consumer interview versus actions, 74
    consumer response to price- and
        sales-related messaging, 72
    cost per thousand (CPM), 75-77
    marketing message sales increase, 66
    marketing technique effectiveness, 64-65
    message impact variance, 67
    message sales lift range, 67
    potential reach, 75-76
    promotion impact, 68-70
    retail marketing effectiveness ratios, 65
    RFID typical placement, 74-75
dump bin effectiveness ratio, 114
dynamic tensions, 215
    consumer dynamic, 216
    retail dynamics
        assortment, 216-217
        communication, 218-219
        familiarity, 218
        navigation, 216-217

E

ease of purchase, 184-185, 205-206
education, 185-186, 206
effectiveness ratio, 29-31, 107, 230
    convenience store study, 55-56
    dump bin effectiveness ratio, 114
    effectiveness ratio without promotional
        message, 115
    effectiveness ratio with promotional
        message, 116
    overall effectiveness ratio, 114
Elizabeth Arden, 155
emotional power, 188-191
engagement factor, 108
engagement model, 138

Envirosell, 161
Estee Lauder, 155
expansive model (ROI), 224-227
expectations, 133
exposure, 80

F–G–H

familiarity, 218
financial impact of presentation optimiza-
    tion, 145-146
focusing attention, 221
frequency of promotions, 37, 80
Frito-Lay, 103, 181

General Mills, 93
general store layout, 157
generic sales increase (convenience store
    study), 53
grocery store layout
    contemporary supermarket layout, 159-160
    traditional grocery store layout, 158-159
Gross Rating Points (GRPs), 80
Group M, 93

HBA category impact ratio, 112
height
    height effectiveness index, 110
    impact by, 110
Hershey's, 103
Hewlett-Packard, 93
holistic marketing scorecard, 15
home pages
    communication/education, 206
    ease of purchase, 205-206
    involvement, 206
    meaningful sites, 209
    overview, 201-202
    page design, 202-203
    page organization, 203
    product access, 204-205
    purchase drivers, 204
    recommended page design, 213
    site navigation, 202
    visibility, 204
Hy-Vee, 93

I

impact by height, 110
impact ratio, 107
    brand A message impact ratio, 113
    HBA category impact ratio, 112
    impact ratio brand comparison, 113
    overall impact ratio, 111
    store material impact ratios, 112
In-Store Marketing Institute (ISMI), 91
In-Store Rating Points (IRP), 80, 82-83
incentives, 210
inconsistent marketing execution, 33-35
industry opportunity (supermarket channel),
    39-40

information overload, 192-193
Integer, 93
integration, 231
interrupting traffic flow, 222
involvement, 187, 206
IRP (In-Store Rating Points), 80, 82-83
ISMI (In-Store Marketing Institute), 91
item tracking (MARI), 109

J–K–L

Kellogg's, 91
Kmart, 93
Korn, Mel, 12
Kraft, 93
Kroger, 15, 91

Lafley, A. G., 97
layers of information in online, 211
layout of stores, 156-163
    chain drug store layout, 158
    contemporary supermarket layout, 159-160
    general store layout, 157
    "race track" layout, 160-161
    Toys R Us, 161-163
    traditional grocery store layout, 158-159
leveraging
    brands, 221-222
    related items
        explained, 177
        purchased drivers. *See* purchase drivers
        shelf alignment, 179-180
        shopper segmentation, 178-179
list use, decline of, 193
logic, 134-138, 198-199
    consumer behavior model, 136
    engagement model, 138
    explained, 134-135
    shopping process, 136-137
L'Oreal, 155

M

MAC (MARI Advisory Council), 103
macroscanning, 171-172
making a stand, 219
managing online dynamics, 207
MARI (Marketing-at-Retail Initiative)
    background, 101-103
    conversion metrics, 108-109
    data delivery, 106
    data summary, 106
    effectiveness ratio, 107
    engagement factor, 108
    impact ratio, 107
    item tracking, 109
    MAC (MARI Advisory Council), 103
    market tests, 103-106
    potential applications, 116-117
    retail marketing ratios, 109-115
    shopping equation, 108

study results, 107
   summary, 117-120
marketing-at-retail activity, 194
Marketing-at-Retail Initiative. *See* MARI
marketing material matrix (supermarket
   study), 28
marketing material observation breakout
   (supermarket study), 29
marketing messages
   comparative price information, 194
   convenience store study, 48-49
   drug store study
      brand-focused messages, 70-71
      category sales response to price/sales
         messaging, 68
      consumer response to price- and
         sales-related messaging, 72
      marketing messages sales increase, 66
      message impact variance, 67
      message sales lift range, 67
   effectiveness ratio, 115
   information overload, 192-193
   shopper exposure to, 94
marketing metrics. *See* metrics
marketing research
   MARI (Marketing-at-Retail Initiative)
      background, 101-103
      conversion metrics, 108-109
      data delivery, 106
      data summary, 106
      effectiveness ratio, 107
      engagement factor, 108
      impact ratio, 107
      item tracking, 109
      MAC (MARI Advisory Council), 103
      market tests, 103-106
      retail marketing ratios, 109-116
      shopping equation, 108
      study results, 107
   Nielsen's PRISM Project
      overview, 89-91
      stage one results, 91-92
      stage two results, 92-93
   Phase One programs
      average sales lift, 87
      average transaction size, 88
      average weekly audience per store, 88
      overview, 85
      retail marketing effectiveness ratio, 87
      retail marketing presense, 86
   POPAI convenience store study
      amount of retail marketing, 53-55
      average brand lift by category, 48
      average coverage by brand category, 45
      core area versus outdoor placement,
         50-51
      cost efficiency, 57-58
      custom versus generic sales increase, 53
      effectiveness ratio impact, 55-56
      key retail marketing location, 46
      marketing messages, 48-49
      outdoor versus indoor lift, 51-52

      overview, 43-44
      percentage of category retail marketing
         by location, 47
      percentage of retail marketing by
         location, 46
      proof of placement, 56-57
      range of sales life, 49-50
      retail marketing placement, 45
      retail marketing techniques, 47
      sales effectiveness, 57-58
      small brand relative sales increase, 52-53
      success element importance by segment,
         58-59
   POPAI drug store study
      brand-focused messages, 70-71
      category sales response to price/sales
         messaging, 68
      compare and save effectiveness ratio,
         72-73
      consumer interview versus actions, 74
      consumer response to price- and
         sales-related messaging, 72
      cost per thousand (CPM), 75-77
      marketing message sales increase, 66
      marketing technique effectiveness, 64-65
      message impact variance, 67
      message sales lift range, 67
      overview, 63-64
      potential reach, 75-76
      promotion impact, 68-70
      retail marketing effectiveness ratios, 65
      RFID typical placement, 74-75
   POPAI supermarket study
      accuracy of measurements, 36-37
      actual audience reach, 82
      brand ROI measurement, 38
      category shopping variations within
         stores, 35-36
      consistent performance areas, 33
      effectiveness of retail marketing, 29-31
      frequency of promotions/size of
         brand, 37
      inconsistent execution, 33-35
      industry opportunity, 39-40
      IRP (In-Store Rating Points), 82-83
      lack of systematic measurement, 38
      marketing material matrix, 28
      marketing material observation
         breakout, 29
      overview, 26-29
      potential reach, 81
      variations in execution and results, 31-33
      timeline, 25-26
market shifts, 2
market tests (MARI), 103-106
MARS Advertising, 93
Mars Snackfood, 93
mass media, 2
Mattel, 19, 93, 156
McDonald, Bob, 92
McKee Foods, 103
meal centers, 185

meaningful conversations, structuring, 220
meaningful sites, 209
Measured Medium Initiative, 25
measurements, 36-37, 223
Measuring At–Retail Advertising
    Effectiveness in Chain Drug
    Stores. *See* drug store study
media integration, 122
media shifts, 2
Meijer, 93, 152
metrics
  accumulation rules for media measures, 80
  audience delivery worksheet, 84-85
    defined, 80
    size of, 94
  conversion metrics, 108-109
  cost per thousand (CPM), 75-77, 79, 83-84
  exposure, 80
  frequency, 80
  Gross Rating Points (GRPs), 80
  In-Store Rating Points (IRP), 80-83
  modeling approach, 93
  Opportunity to See (OTS), 79
  overview, 79
  reach, 80-82
  recency theory, 80
  Target Rating Points (TRPs), 80
Miller Brewing, 91
modeling approach, 93
Moore's Law, 1
multiplatform strategy, 209

N–O

navigating home pages, 202
navigation, 156-163, 216-217
Nielsen's PRISM Project
  overview, 89-91
  stage one results, 91-92
  stage two results, 92-93
Nintendo, 93

OMD, 93
online retailing
  connection/involvement with shoppers, 212
  data analysis, 211
  dominant shopper patterns, 208-209
  home pages
    communication/education, 206
    ease of purchase, 205-206
    involvement, 206
    meaningful sites, 209
    overview, 201-202
    page design, 202-203
    page organization, 203
    product access, 204-205
    purchase drivers, 204
    recommended page design, 213
    site navigation, 202
    visibility, 204
  incentives, 210

layers of information, 211
multiplatform strategy, 209
online dynamics, managing, 207
overview, 197
path to purchase, 212
personalization, 209-210
search optimization, 208
shopper behavior
  biologic, 200
  cognitive research, 197-198
  decision drivers, 200-206
  logic, 198-199
  social influences, 199-200
operating within dominant shopper
  schemata, 220
opportunities, shaping, 187-188
Opportunity to See (OTS), 79
optimizing searches (online retailing), 208
organizing
  home pages, 203
  store shelves
    dominant brand on lowest shelf, 172
    dominant brand side by side, 173
    importance of, 175-176
    macroscanning, 171-172
    physical arrangement examples, 168-170
    section organization, 176-177
    shopper focus, 173-174
    vertical segmentation, 175
OTS (Opportunity to See), 79
outdoor placement, 50-51
overall effectiveness ratio, 114
overall evaluation model (ROI), 227
overall impact ratio, 111

P

pages. *See* home pages
Pathmark, 93
path to purchase, 212
patterns, 95-96, 129-131, 208-209, 220
Pepsi, 103
perceived risk, 137
perception, influence of display organization
  on, 194
personal accounting, 137
personalization, 209-210
Phase One programs
  average sales lift, 87
  average transaction size, 88
  average weekly audience per store, 88
  overview, 85
  retail marketing effectiveness ratio, 87
  retail marketing presense, 86
Phillips, Hugh, 126, 128, 171-173
physical arrangement examples (shelf
  organization), 168-170
Pioneering Research for an In-Store Metric.
  See PRISM Project
planned versus unplanned purchases,
  148-150
PolyTrack video analysis, 105

POPAI
    convenience store study, 43-59
    drug store study, 63-78
    MARI (Marketing at Retail Initiative)
        background, 101-103
        conversion metrics, 108-109
        data delivery, 106
        data summary, 106
        effectiveness ratio, 107
        engagement factor, 108
        impact ratio, 107
        item tracking, 109
        MAC (MARI Advisory Council), 103
        market tests, 103-106
        potential applications, 116-117
        retail marketing ratios, 109-116
        shopping equation, 108
        study results, 107
        summary, 117-120
    Measured Medium Initiative
    supermarket study, 26-40
        actual audience reach, 82
        IRP (In-Store Rating Points), 82-83
        potential reach, 81
potential applications (MARI), 116-117
potential reach, 75-76, 81
The Power of Marketing at Retail
    (Phillips), 128
presentation optimization, financial impact
    of, 145-146
Price Chopper, 93
Prime Consulting Group, 79
PRISM (Pioneering Research for an In-Store
    Metric) Project
    overview, 89-91
    stage one results, 91-92
    stage two results, 92-93
Procter & Gamble, 91
product access in home pages, 204-205
product as visual billboard, 183
promotions
    frequency of, 37
    impact, 68-70
proof of placement, 56-57
psychographic segmentation, 20-23
purchase drivers, 204. *See also* decision drivers
    access, 183
    ease of purchase, 184-185
    education, 185-186
    explained, 180-181
    involvement, 187
    purchase driver matrix, 188
    shaping opportunities, 187-188
    visibility, 181-183

Q–R

"race track" layout, 160-161
reach
    actual audience reach, 82
    defined, 80
    potential reach, 81

REAP (Retail Ecosystem Analytics
    Process), 152
    analysis, 8
    assortment, 8
    case studies
        brand channel segmentation, 19
        collaborative failure, 18-19
        retailer assortment rationalization, 17-18
        shopper psychographic segmentation,
            20-23
    constituency inclusion, 9-12
    design, 9
    design process, 3
    overview, 1-7
    shopper analysis integration
        explained, 12-14
        retail marketing scorecards, 14-15
        segmentation premiums, 15-16
        traditional shopper segmentation traits,
            16-17
    structure, 8-9
recency theory, 80
refining plans, 223
related items, leveraging
    explained, 177
    purchase drivers. *See* purchase drivers
    shelf alignment, 179-180
    shopper segmentation, 178-179
relaxation, 192
research. *See* marketing research
retail dynamics
    assortment, 216-217
    communication, 218-219
    familiarity, 218
    navigation, 216-217
Retail Ecosystem Analytics Process.
    See REAP
retail factors and purchase decision
    types, 145
retail marketing model shift, 120-124
    best practices model, 122
    discourse shift, 121
    media integration, 122
    retail marketing model, 123
retail marketing presense, 86
retail marketing ratios, 109
    brand A message impact ratio, 113
    drug store study, 65
    dump bin effectiveness ratio, 114
    effectiveness ratio without promotional
        message, 115
    effectiveness ratio with promotional
        message, 115
    HBA category impact ratio, 112
    height effectiveness index, 110
    impact by height, 110
    impact ratio brand comparison, 113
    overall effectiveness ratio, 114
    overall impact ratio, 111
    Phase One programs, 87
    store material impact ratios, 112
retail marketing scorecards, 14-15

retail maturation, 2
retail model (ROI), 228-229
retail success drivers
    adjacencies, 165-168
    assortment, 163-164
    color palette, 154-156
    decision steps and drivers, 149-151
    explained, 150
    shelf organization, 168-177
    store exterior, 151-154
    store layout/navigation, 156-163
retail success dynamic, 146-148
retailer acceptance scorecard, 15
retailer assortment rationalization (case study), 17-18
return on investment. *See* ROI
RFID typical placement, 74-75
Rite Aid, 93. *See also* drug store study
ROI (return on investment)
    analytic brand model, 228
    analytic retail model, 227
    expansive model, 224-227
    explained, 38, 223
    overall evaluation model, 227
    retail model, 228-229
    traditional model, 223-224

S

Safeway, 93, 103
sales effectiveness, 57-58
sales lift
    convenience store study
        outdoor versus indoor lift, 51-52
        range of sales life, 49-50
    drug store study, 67, 71
    Phase One programs, 87
Schnucks, 93
Schultz, Howard, 120
search optimization, 208
Sears, 93
section organization, 176-177
segmentation
    brand channel segmentation, 19
    segmentation premiums, 15-16
    shopper psychographic segmentation, 20-23
    shopper segmentation, 178-179
    snack aisle segmentation, 181-182
    traditional shopper segmentation traits, 16-17
    vertical segmentation, 175
selective perception, 129
7-Eleven, 103
shaping opportunities, 187-188
shelf alignment, 179-180
shelf organization
    dominant brand on lowest shelf, 172
    dominant brand side by side, 173
    importance of, 175-176
    macroscanning, 171-172
    physical arrangement examples, 168-170

section organization, 176-177
    shopper focus, 173-174
    vertical segmentation, 175
Sheridan Global Consulting, 103
shift in retail marketing model, 120-124
    best practices model, 122
    discourse shift, 121
    media integration, 122
    retail marketing model, 123
ShopConsult, 154, 172
shopper analysis integration
    explained, 12-14
    retail marketing scorecards, 14-15
    segmentation premiums, 15-16
    traditional shopper segmentation traits, 16-17
shopper behavior
    biologic, 141-143, 200
    boredom, 141
    cognitive research, 126, 197-198
    conscious processing, 128-129
    consistency, 131-134, 141
    consumer behavior model, 136
    consumer dynamic, 216
    consumer interview versus actions, 74
    consumer response to price- and sales-related messaging, 72
    decision drivers, 200-201
    deselection, 127-128
    explained, 126
    focus, 173-174
    logic, 134-138, 198-199
        consumer behavior model, 136
        explained, 134-135
    pattern and structures, 129-131
    selective perception, 129
    shopper stimulation, 143
    social influences, 138-141, 199-200
shopper direction, 192
shopper psychographic segmentation, 20-23
shopper relevancy scorecard, 14
shopper segmentation, 178-179
shopper stimulation, 143
shopping equation, 108
shopping process, 136-137
Simons, Daniel, 127
site navigation, 202
size of retail audience, 94
small brand relative sales increase (convenience store study), 52
snack aisle segmentation, 181-182
social influences, 138-141, 199-200
stage one results (PRISM), 91-92
stage two results (PRISM), 92-93
Starbucks, 120
Starcom MediaVest, 93
stimulation, 143
Stop & Shop, 93
store exteriors, 151-154
store layout/navigation, 156-163
    chain drug store layout, 158
    contemporary supermarket layout, 159-160

general store layout, 157
influence on traffic patterns, 96
"race track" layout, 160-161
Toys R Us, 161-163
traditional grocery store layout, 158-159
store material impact ratios, 112
structures, 8-9, 129-131
success element importance by segment
(convenience store study), 58-59
supermarket layout
contemporary supermarket layout, 159-160
traditional grocery store layout, 158-159
supermarket study (POPAI), 26-29
accuracy of measurements, 36-37
actual audience reach, 82
brand ROI measurement, 38
category shopping variations within stores,
35-36
consistent performance areas, 33
effectiveness of retail marketing, 29-31
frequency of promotions/size of brand, 37
inconsistent execution, 33-35
industry opportunity, 38-40
IRP (In-Store Rating Points), 82-83
marketing material matrix, 28
marketing material observation
breakout, 29
potential reach, 81
variations in execution and results, 31-33
Supervalu, 93
systematic measurement, lack of, 38

T

Target, 93, 130
Target Rating Points (TRPs), 80
theft deterrents, 185
3M, 91
timeline of marketing research, 25-26
tools for retail success
adjacencies, 221
choosing when to interrupt traffic flow, 222
complementary merchandising, 220
consistent execution, 222
focusing attention, 221
leveraging brands, 221-222
making a stand, 219
meaningful conversations, 220
measuring and refining, 223
operating within dominant shopper
schemata, 220
shopper intimacy, 229-233

Toys R Us, 161-163
traditional grocery store layout, 158-159
traditional model (ROI), 223-224
traditional shopper segmentation traits, 16-17
traffic
choosing when to interrupt traffic flow, 222
fluctuations in, 96
influence of store design on, 96
volume versus traffic, 94
transaction size, 88
TRPs (Target Rating Points), 80

U-V

Underhill, Paco, 161
Unilever, 93, 103

variations in marketing execution and results,
31-33
vertical segmentation, 175
visibility, 181-183, 204
visual billboard, product as, 183
volume versus traffic, 94
Vons, 153

W-X-Y-Z

Walgreens, 91, 103. *See also* drug store study
Walmart, 91, 152
Walt Disney Company, 91
Wanamaker, John, 6
Weber's Law, 137
weekly audience per store (Phase One
programs), 88
Whetstone, Don, 103
Whole Food, 15, 183
Winn-Dixie, 93
Wishart, George, 90